GINO'S HIDDEN ITALY

GINO D'ACAMPO

HOW TO COOK LIKE A TRUE ITALIAN

HODDER &
STOUGHTON

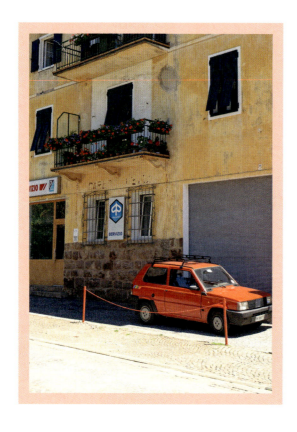

First published in Great Britain in 2016 by Hodder & Stoughton

An Hachette UK company

1

Copyright © ITV Ventures Ltd 2016

Recipes copyright © Gino D'Acampo Ltd 2016

Television series *Gino's Italian Escape: Hidden Italy* copyright © ITV Studios Limited 2016. Licensed by ITV Ventures Ltd. All rights reserved.

Recipe photography by Matt Russell 2016

Additional recipe photography by Dan Jones 2016: pages 32, 52, 57, 88, 93, 95, 166

Italy photography and endpaper photography by Hal Shinnie 2016

Additional photography copyright © Shutterstock. com: pages 61 (bottom right), 136 (bottom left), 210 (top right)

Map by Tom Woolley

A CIP catalogue record for this title is available from the British Library

Hardback ISBN 978 1 473 64648 3

Ebook ISBN 978 1 473 64649 0

Editorial Director: Nicky Ross
Editor: Polly Boyd
Project Editor: Kate Miles
Design excluding cover: Georgia Vaux
Photographers: Matt Russell, Hal Shinnie and Dan Jones
Food Stylist: Gee Charman
Food styling assistants: Tamara Vos and Leonie Sooke
Props Stylist: Lydia Brun
Props styling assistant: Lauren Miller
Shoot Producer: Ruth Ferrier
Proofreader: Miren Lopategui
Indexer: Hilary Bird

Typeset in Halis Grotesque
Printed and bound by Firmengruppe APPL, aprinta druck, Wemding, Germany

Hodder & Stoughton policy is to use papers that are natural, renewable and recyclable products and made from wood grown in sustainable forests. The logging and manufacturing processes are expected to conform to the environmental regulations of the country of origin.

Hodder & Stoughton Ltd
Carmelite House
50 Victoria Embankment
London EC4Y 0DZ
www.hodder.co.uk

ITALY'S REGIONI

AUSTRIA

SWITZERLAND

HUNGARY

VAL D'AOSTA

TRENTINO-ALTO ADIGE

FRIULI-VENEZIA GIULIA

SLOVENIA

CROATIA

LOMBARDY

VENETO

MILAN

VENICE

BOSNIA AND HERZEGOVINA

TURIN

PIEDMONT

EMILIA-ROMAGNA

LIGURIA

BOLOGNA

GENOA

FRANCE

LIGURIAN SEA

FLORENCE

CORSICA

TUSCANY

MARCHE

UMBRIA

PESCARA

ADRIATIC SEA

LAZIO

ABRUZZO

ROME

MOLISE

CAMPANIA

BARI

PUGLIA

NAPLES

BASILICATA

SARDINIA

CALABRIA

CAGLIARI

TYRRHENIAN SEA

PALERMO

MEDITERRANEAN SEA

SICILY

IONIAN SEA

Although I visited quite a few places in northern and central Italy for the first series of *Gino's Italian Escape* I came away feeling that I had 'unfinished business' – I'd loved it so much yet felt that I had only scratched the surface. So I decided to return and delve deeper to find the hidden gems – exploring out-of-the-way places, chatting with the locals and discovering amazing traditional dishes and fresh seasonal produce.

Non-Italians often think of Italy as one country with a single identity, culture and cuisine, but really it's a collection of regions. Each of the 20 *regioni* (which were independent states until Italy's unification in the mid-19th century) have very distinct characteristics, with ingredients and cooking varying enormously from one region to another. My trip began in Lombardy – Milan and Lake Como – and from there we travelled to Piedmont (*Piemonte*), Liguria and Trentino-Alto Adige in the north and Tuscany (*Toscana*), Umbria and Abruzzo in the central part of the country. The regions were all so different from one another – and of course different again from southern Italy, where I come from.

Northern Italy

The cuisines of Lombardy and Piedmont – in the northwest of the country – are dominated by rice. You won't be able to visit these regions without some kind of risotto dish being offered to you, which is why I've devoted a whole chapter to it in this book – it's even more popular than pasta. With over 4,000 rice growers in the country, Italy is Europe's largest rice producer, with most of it cultivated in the Po Valley – a major geographical feature in northern Italy stretching about 70,000 square kilometres from the French border in the west to the Adriatic Sea in the east. Irrigation is provided by mountain streams, and if you visit in May you'll find the rice fields submerged in water. Butter and cheese are also very popular in these regions, and Piedmont has the added bonus of producing the most wonderful truffles, including the renowned white truffle – the world's most expensive food. If you go to Piedmont please try the *fonduta* – a dip made of melted fontina cheese served with truffles – *da morire*!

To the northeast lies the mountainous region of Trentino-Alto Adige. This region has an unusual history as it is really two distinct areas – the upper part (Alto Adige, also known as the South Tyrol) was part of Austria until World War I and so German language, food and culture predominate, while Trentino in the south is more typically Italian, with a cuisine like that enjoyed in Veneto.

Cheeses are very important in this region and I sampled a huge range when I visited. I even turned my hand to making caciotta al timo – a cow's milk cheese flavoured with thyme. Cured meats are also popular, with speck (a kind of smoked prosciutto) being a real highlight for me. Another regional speciality is dumplings (known as *canederli* in Trentino and *knödel* in Alto Adige), which are put in soups, served with a sauce or as a dessert. Much of the bread is quite different from elsewhere in Italy – darker and heavier, as rye flour is often combined with wheat flour – and the Austrian-style cakes are out of this world. I've included an apple strudel and an apple and rosemary cake in this book, both of which are inspired by the region's incredible *pasticcerie* (patisseries).

Liguria has a very different culinary history. Consisting of a rugged, narrow strip between the mountains and the sea, the land is unsuited to grain growing and pastureland. Instead, the Ligurians have created steep terraced gardens where they cultivate a huge array of amazing vegetables, herbs and olives. Vegetables are at the centre of Ligurian cuisine, as is olive oil, and some of the world's best olive oil is made here. Historically, potatoes and potato bread have also played an important role in the Ligurian diet, and if you haven't yet tasted potato bread you're in for a treat – try my recipe and you'll be amazed by its rich flavour and moist texture. Along the coast there is abundant fresh fish from the Gulf of Genoa, and tuna-stuffed fennel and stuffed squid (both featured in this book) are among the many excellent seafood dishes I enjoyed in Liguria.

Central Italy

Although it is one of the most visited regions of Italy, Tuscany still has plenty of hidden gems. Its cuisine is renowned throughout the world yet the best meals I experienced there were the simplest – served in rustic restaurants in the most unexpected places and in people's homes. Much of the food is centred around meat – *bistecca* (grilled steak), roast pork, and chicken and rabbit casseroles. The Tuscans are great hunters, and wild boar and game are enjoyed in season. Hearty soups are also a key part of the diet – one of the favourites being *ribollita*, made from vegetables, beans and stale bread, flavoured with olive oil. I love it so much that I simply had to include it here.

Olive oil is also a key element of the cuisine in neighbouring Umbria and it permeates local dishes with its distinctive flavour. Umbria is particularly famous for its pork products – sausages, salamis and cured hams – and *porchetta* (spit-roasted suckling pig), which is served at markets and village celebrations. Beef, lamb, game and fish are also popular. The small beige-green Umbrian lentils – sweet and full of flavour – are considered the best in Italy and they inspired me to create a new recipe: a lentil and squash salad. But perhaps the greatest delicacy of the region is the black truffle, found near Norcia, which transforms ordinary dishes such as pasta or *frittata* into heavenly meals.

Abruzzo, on the Adriatic coast, was my southernmost destination on this trip. Extremely mountainous, this region was cut off from the rest of Italy for centuries, with the inhabitants (mainly shepherds, farmers and fishermen)

traditionally leading tough, solitary lives. In fact until 14 years ago there wasn't an airport in the region, so it really is 'hidden Italy' – relatively undiscovered and untainted by tourism, despite its glorious beaches. The diet in Abruzzo is based largely on lamb and pork (inland) and fish (on the coast). The style of cooking is similar to that found in southern Italy – pasta is very popular, with *spaghetti alla chitarra* (which I learned to make the traditional way) a speciality of the region – and dishes tend to be highly spiced with chillies.

Local farms and food festivals

Although Italy has many wonderful cities that are rich in culture, I like nothing better than to head off to the countryside to seek out small family-run farms where they make their own produce – honey, olive oil, bread, cheeses, salamis and many other regional specialities. All made on site, these foods are the essence of rural Italy – beautiful, simple food in stunning surroundings.

I also love visiting food fairs or festivals. For instance, the world-famous Truffle Festival in Alba, Piedmont, which I went to in October with the TV crew. If you get a chance to go, please do – it's an absolute must. What struck me most was how people from all walks of life – whether a top chef, truffle connoisseur or a grandma from down the road – would give each other time, talking, sharing and learning about food – it really was a food-lover's dream. Of course, I had to include some truffle recipes in this book – expensive, but so worth it for a treat.

Throughout the country there are also hundreds of smaller, more local regional food festivals known as *sagre*. Originally these were religious fairs (*sagre* derives from *sacra*, meaning sacred), but in recent decades they have become secular events – usually dedicated to one local ingredient or dish. If you're visiting Italy I really recommend you look out for any *sagre* in your area (you'll see colourful posters advertising the events around towns and on the roadsides). Lasting anything from a weekend to ten days, they're a fantastic opportunity to taste local seasonal foods, often in a beautiful small town or village that is well off the beaten track. They're also a great way to experience the 'real' Italy – sitting side by side with the locals at a long shared table to eat, drink and enjoy live music and traditional community entertainment.

I learned so much from my trip around northern and central Italy. I tried all sorts of exciting dishes that I hadn't tried before and learned to use familiar ingredients in completely different ways. This book is the result of my amazing culinary journey – it combines dishes that are both traditional and typical of the regions I visited as well as new creations that were inspired by the trip. I really hope you enjoy them as much as I do.

Buon appetito!

Gino xxx

REGIONAL SAGRE

Below is just a small selection of *sagre* (food festivals) in the northern and central regions that we visited when filming in Italy.

PASTA, GNOCCHI, POLENTA & RISOTTO

Spaghetti alla chitarra Castelnuovo al Vomano (Abruzzo), July
Pizzoccheri (buckwheat pasta) Teglio (Lombardy), July and September
Gnocchi Terni (Umbria), July
Polenta Bregnano (Lombardy), September
Risotto Villimpenta (Lombardy), June

CHEESE & CURED MEATS

Gorgonzola Gorgonzola (Lombardy), September
Grana Padano Goito (Lombardy), October
Provolone Cremona (Lombardy), June
Taleggio Ballabio (Lombardy), April
Bresaola Sondria (Lombardy), May
Prosciutto (cured ham) Norcia (Umbria), October–November
Speck (cured smoked ham) Santa Maddalena (Trentino-Alto Adige), October

FRESH MEAT & FISH

Bistecca (grilled T-bone steak) Cortona (Tuscany), August
Frog and snail (*ranocchiocciola*) Massarosa (Tuscany), July
Goose (*oca*) Mortara (Lombardy), September
Porchetta (roasted suckling pig) Campli (Abruzzo), August
Wild boar (*cinghiale*) Pergo (Tuscany), July
Fish (*pesce*) Camogli (Liguria), May
Lake fish: fresh (*agone*), preserved (*missoltino*) Tremezzina (Lombardy), August
Sardine (*sardina*) Gallinarga (Lombardy), July

VEGETABLES, MUSHROOMS & TRUFFLES

Asparagus and artichoke (*asparago e carciofo*) Loano (Liguria), April
Aubergine (*melanzana*) Castiglione Chiavara (Liguria), August
Broad bean (*baccello*) Salviano (Tuscany), May

Chicory (*cicoria*) Cazzano Sant'Andrea (Lombardy), May
Chilli (*peperoncino*) Chieti (Abruzzo), August
Courgette (*zucchina*) Giove (Umbria), July
Garlic (*aglio*) Vessalico (Liguria), July
Lentil (*lenticchie*) Castelluccio di Norcia (Umbria), August
Onion (*cipolla*) Cannara (Umbria), September
Pepper (*peperone*) Carmagnola (Piedmont), August–September
Potato (*patata*) Neirone (Liguria), August
Pumpkin (*zucca*) Piegaia (Tuscany), October
Wild mushroom (*fungo porcino*) Cortona (Tuscany), August
Black truffle (*tartufo nero*) Norcia (Umbria), February–March
Black summer truffle (*scorzone*) San Venanzo (Umbria), July–August
White truffle (*tartufo bianco*) Alba and Moncalvo (Piedmont), October–November

FRUIT & NUTS

Cherry (*ciliegia*) Lari (Tuscany), May–June
Chestnut (*castagna*) Marradi (Tuscany), October
Grape (*uva*) Impruneta (Tuscany), September
Hazelnut (*nocciola*) Cortemilia (Piedmont), August
Lemon (*limone*) Monterosso (Liguria), May

BREAD & SWEET THINGS

Focaccia Recco (Liguria), May
Rye and spelt bread Bressanone (Trentino-Alto Adige), October
Canederli (dumplings) Vipiteno (Trentino-Alto Adige), September
Chocolate (*cioccolato*) Turin (Piedmont), November
Honey (*miele*) Montalcino (Tuscany), September
Strudel Bressanone (Trentino-Alto Adige), October

The north of Italy offers a wonderful selection of antipasti – so much so they are often my favourite part of the meal. Near the lakes and on the coast many starters consist of fish and other seafood, but if you travel towards the mountains you'll find cheeses, cured meats, mushrooms and hearty, wholesome soups on the menu.

ANTIPASTI & SOUPS

APERITIVO: ROASTED PEACH BELLINI COCKTAIL WITH OLIVE BALLS

Bellini con pesche al forno e bocconcini alle olive, formaggio e noci

SERVES 6

For the olive balls
250g full-fat cream
  cheese (chilled)
125g soft goat's cheese
  (chilled)
2 tablespoons fresh
  thyme leaves
12 pitted black olives,
  drained
100g roasted unsalted
  peanuts, chopped
Salt and freshly ground
  black pepper

For the cocktail
4 white peaches
1 x 750ml bottle of
  prosecco (chilled)

Italians love to start the evening with an *aperitivo*, or pre-dinner drink. It whets the appetite and provides the perfect opportunity to relax and socialise after a day's work. Whether you're in a bar or at someone's home, *aperitivi* are always served with nibbles, ranging from simple olives to generous platters of *antipasti*. This famous Peach Bellini cocktail was created in Harry's Bar in Venice in the 1930s. The recipe is meant to be a closely guarded secret, but a few years ago I managed to inveigle the recipe from one of the barmaids – so here it is, with an accompanying snack of delicious crunchy little olive balls. *Salute!*

1. First make the olive balls. In a chilled bowl mix together the cream cheese, goat's cheese and thyme until well combined. Season with salt and pepper.

2. Take a teaspoonful of the cheese mixture and pack it around the outside of each olive until completely coated. Roll each ball in the peanuts and place on a serving platter. Cover and refrigerate.

3. To make the cocktail, preheat the oven to 180°C/gas mark 4. Place the peaches on a baking sheet and roast for 25–30 minutes or until softened. Leave to cool. Slice in half then remove and discard the skin and stones.

4. Transfer the peach flesh to a blender or food processor and purée until smooth, then push the pulp through a fine sieve set over a bowl.

5. Spoon 2–3 teaspoons of the mixture into a champagne flute then carefully pour over the prosecco. Stir well and serve immediately with the olive balls.

Crostini con mozzarella, prosciutto, fichi e miele

SERVES 4-6

12 slices of ciabatta,
   about 1cm thick
3 tablespoons extra
   virgin olive oil
3 x 125g balls of
   mozzarella, drained
6 slices of Parma ham
6 ripe figs
2 tablespoons runny
   honey

Affectionately known as 'pigs and figs' in my house, this is a really simple and delicious first course or light lunch if served with a green salad. The sweet flavour and luscious texture of fresh figs combines perfectly with the salty Parma ham and creamy mozzarella. Many different types of figs are grown in Italy. The peak season for the purple-black varieties is usually late August to early September, but some green kinds are available earlier.

1. Preheat the grill for about 5 minutes to medium high. Brush both sides of the ciabatta with the oil and place the slices on a large baking sheet. Grill for 1–2 minutes each side or until just golden. The bread can be grilled up to 1 day ahead and will keep crisp if stored in an airtight container.

2. Preheat the oven to 200°C/gas mark 6. Cut each ball of mozzarella into four slices. Slice each piece of ham in half crossways. Top the crostini with a slice each of mozzarella and ham.

3. Bake the crostini for 5 minutes or until the mozzarella starts to soften and the ham starts to crisp. Meanwhile, halve the figs.

4. Arrange the crostini on a large serving platter. Top each with a fig half and drizzle with the honey. Serve immediately.

GRILLED PEPPERS WITH CHERRY TOMATOES, OLIVES AND CAPERS

Peperoni grigliati con pomodorini, olive e capperi

SERVES 6

3 red peppers, halved
  lengthways, cored
  and deseeded
3 yellow peppers,
  halved lengthways,
  cored and deseeded
Olive oil for brushing
200g fresh red cherry
  tomatoes, quartered
50g pitted black olives
  (preferably Taggiasca),
  drained

For the dressing
1 garlic clove
1 tablespoon capers,
  drained
4 tablespoons chopped
  fresh flat-leaf parsley
4 tablespoons chopped
  fresh oregano
4 tablespoons snipped
  fresh chives
100ml extra virgin
  olive oil
Salt and freshly ground
  black pepper

Sweet red and yellow peppers grow all over Italy, but the best ones are from Umbria and Piedmont – which is where this colourful rustic dish originates. If you like spice, stir in some dried chilli flakes before adding the dressing. Serve with toasted ciabatta rubbed with a peeled garlic clove.

1. Preheat the grill for about 5 minutes to medium high. Line a large baking sheet with foil. Place the peppers, cut-side down, on the baking sheet and brush with a little olive oil. Grill for 15 minutes or until the skins blister and are blackened.

2. Transfer the peppers to a large plastic food bag, seal and leave to cool for about 20 minutes (this traps steam, which will help loosen the skin from the flesh, making the peppers easier to peel). Peel off the skins and slice or tear the peppers into long strips.

3. Place the peppers in a large, shallow serving bowl and add the tomatoes and olives.

4. To make the dressing, bruise the garlic by placing it under the flat side of a knife and pressing down with your palm to crush it slightly, then peel. Put the clove in a small bowl, add the capers and herbs and stir in the oil. Season with salt and pepper.

5. Pour the dressing over the peppers, tomatoes and olives and mix until evenly coated. Discard the garlic. Serve at room temperature.

DEEP-FRIED COURGETTE FLOWERS STUFFED WITH RICOTTA   21

Fiori di zucchine fritti e ripieni di ricotta

SERVES 6

12 courgette flowers
250g ricotta cheese
25g Grana Padano
  cheese, finely grated
Grated zest of ½
  unwaxed lemon
About 1 litre of
  sunflower oil for
  deep-frying
Sea salt flakes and
  freshly ground
  black pepper

For the batter
300g plain flour
1 x 7g sachet fast-
  action (easy blend)
  dried yeast
Pinch of salt
1 egg yolk
500ml Italian beer
  (lager)

Courgette flowers, sold in bunches in Italian markets in midsummer, are usually a privilege reserved for the kitchen gardener in Britain. They're a rare treat in the shops, so if you see courgette flowers for sale snap them up and cook them the same day – they don't last long. For variety, add some fresh mint to the ricotta mixture or pop in a small cube of mozzarella.

1. First make the batter. Place the flour in a large bowl with the yeast and salt. Make a well in the centre and add the egg yolk. Pour in the beer, a little at a time, whisking until the flour is completely blended and the mixture is smooth. Cover with cling film and leave to rest for 1½ hours at room temperature.

2. Meanwhile, using your fingers, gently part the courgette flower petals and remove and discard the stamens. Set the flowers aside.

3. To make the filling, put the ricotta, Grana Padano and lemon zest in a medium bowl. Stir to combine and season with salt and pepper. Carefully stuff each flower with about 1 tablespoon of the cheese mixture. Be careful not to over-fill. To seal, bring the petals together to enclose the mixture and twist the ends slightly.

4. Heat a deep-fat fryer to 180°C, or heat the oil in a deep pan or a wok until very hot. To test the temperature, drop a teaspoon of the batter into the oil; it will sizzle when the oil is hot enough for frying.

5. Dip each stuffed courgette flower into the batter and transfer to the hot oil to deep-fry for 2–3 minutes or until golden brown and crispy. You will need to fry in batches of 2 at a time so they are not touching. Carefully remove the flowers with tongs or a slotted spoon and drain on kitchen paper. Sprinkle over some sea salt flakes and a few grindings of pepper and serve immediately.

GOAT'S CHEESE, GREEN BEAN, PINE NUT AND EGG SALAD

Insalata allegria

SERVES 6-8

8 medium free-range eggs
200g fine green beans, trimmed
100g rocket leaves
100g baby spinach leaves
100g ruby gem lettuce, roughly chopped
300g soft goat's cheese
50g toasted pine nuts, roughly chopped

For the dressing
2 tablespoons runny honey
Juice of 1 lemon
200ml extra virgin olive oil
Salt and freshly ground black pepper

Italy produces many types of goat's cheese, mainly in the northern Alpine regions of the Val d'Aosta, Piedmont, Lombardy, Trentino-Alto Adige, Friuli-Venezia Giulia and Veneto. I've used a soft goat's cheese for this recipe, but you could just as easily use a drier, more crumbly type, and substitute walnuts for the pine nuts. Serve with grissini or crusty bread.

1. First hard-boil the eggs. Place a medium pan of water on the hob and bring to the boil. Carefully lower the eggs into the pan, bring the water back to the boil then reduce the heat to a gentle simmer and cook for 10 minutes. Lift out the eggs and plunge them into a bowl of cold water. Peel when they are cool enough to handle. Leave to cool then slice lengthways into quarters.

2. Bring a small saucepan of salted water to the boil. Tip in the beans, reduce the heat, cover and simmer for 3 minutes. Drain in a colander and rinse with very cold water (so they retain their colour and crunch), then drain again. Leave to cool then chop the beans into short lengths.

3. To make the dressing, put the honey and lemon juice in a small bowl and stir to combine. Whisk in the oil gradually and season with salt and pepper.

4. Arrange the rocket, spinach and lettuce leaves on a large serving platter. Dot with the goat's cheese and scatter over the beans and pine nuts. Pour most of the dressing over the salad and toss together.

5. Place the eggs on top of the salad. Grind pepper over the top and drizzle over the remaining dressing.

Insalata con brasato

SERVES 6

2 tablespoons olive oil
1kg silverside of beef
10 cloves
1 onion, peeled and
  halved
3 celery sticks, cut
  into chunks
1 large carrot, peeled
  and cut into chunks
4 bay leaves
2 tablespoons brandy
2 fresh tomatoes,
  scored at the base
1 teaspoon salt

For the salad
1 large cos lettuce,
  leaves separated
3 fresh plum tomatoes,
  roughly chopped
3 celery sticks, finely
  sliced
Handful (about 25g) of
  chopped fresh flat-
  leaf parsley
1 fresh, medium-hot
  red chilli, deseeded
  and finely sliced
2 tablespoons extra
  virgin olive oil, plus
  extra for drizzling
1 tablespoon red wine
  vinegar
Salt and freshly ground
  black pepper

Beef is a favourite in northern Italy, where much of the land is pasture and cows graze naturally on grass to produce leaner meat with great flavour. Beef salads – sometimes using raw meat – are popular in the region. For this recipe I have used cooked silverside, as I like the flavour and think it's good value for money, but feather or chuck steak would work just as well.

1. Heat the oil in a large flameproof casserole over a medium to high heat. When very hot, add the beef and fry for about 1 minute each side until browned. Remove with a slotted spoon and transfer to a large plate. Set aside.

2. Reduce the heat to medium. Press the cloves into the onion halves and add to the casserole, then add the celery, carrot and bay leaves. Fry gently for about 5 minutes, stirring occasionally.

3. Increase the heat and pour in the brandy. Bring to the boil and let it bubble for about 30 seconds. Return the beef to the pan and add the tomatoes and salt. Pour over enough cold water to cover the meat (about 4 litres). Bring to the boil then reduce the heat and simmer for 30 minutes. Skim off any froth from the surface using a slotted spoon. Cover and simmer for a further 2–2½ hours or until the meat is tender.

4. Lift the meat from the liquid and transfer to a board. Strain the cooking liquid into a large bowl and discard the vegetables and bay leaves. You can use the liquid as stock for another dish (it will freeze well). When the beef has cooled slightly, but is still warm, shred the meat with your fingers.

5. Put the lettuce, plum tomatoes, celery, parsley and chilli in a large bowl. Add the oil and vinegar and season with salt and pepper. Toss well to combine.

6. Transfer the salad to a large serving platter. Pile the shredded beef on top and drizzle with additional oil.

COD SALAD WITH ROASTED NEW POTATOES AND OLIVES

Insalata di merluzzo con patate arrosto e olive

SERVES 4

150g sea salt flakes
1 bay leaf
10 pink peppercorns
3 juniper berries
500g cod fillet
  (skin on), pin-boned
450g baby new
  potatoes, scrubbed
3 tablespoons olive oil
50g pitted black olives
  (preferably Leccino),
  drained
l sprig of fresh oregano
3 spring onions (white
  part sliced across,
  green part sliced
  lengthways into
  fine strips)
1 fresh, medium-hot
  red chilli, deseeded
  and finely sliced
1 tablespoon chopped
  fresh flat-leaf parsley

For the dressing
1 teaspoon runny
  honey
1 tablespoon lemon
  juice
1 tablespoon white
  wine vinegar
70ml extra virgin
  olive oil
Salt and freshly ground
  black pepper

This lively salad was one of my absolute favourites when I was a child and brings back happy memories of my mother making it for our lunch in the long, hot summers. Fresh cod is popular in Italy, but dried salt cod (*baccalà*) – traditionally eaten on Christmas Eve – is more common in non-coastal areas. Serve with crusty bread and Grilled Peppers (see page 18).

1. Put 1 litre of cold water in a medium saucepan. Add the salt, bay leaf, peppercorns and juniper berries. Bring to the boil then remove from the heat and leave to cool. Squeeze the juniper berries to release their flavour, drop them back into the pan, then add the cod. Cover and leave to stand at room temperature for 3 hours. To make the dressing, whisk together the honey, lemon juice, vinegar and extra virgin olive oil and season with salt and pepper. Set aside.

2. Preheat the oven to 200°C/gas mark 6. Put the potatoes in a baking dish, pour over 2 tablespoons of the olive oil and stir to coat. Roast for 15 minutes, then add the olives and roast for a further 20 minutes. Remove from the oven (but leave it on) and set aside to cool.

3. Transfer the fish to a board or large plate and pat dry with kitchen paper. Discard the soaking liquid and flavourings. Line a roasting tin with baking parchment, allowing extra parchment to cover the fish.

4. Heat the remaining 1 tablespoon of oil in a medium frying pan over a high heat. When hot, add the oregano then the cod. Fry the fish for 1 minute each side or until lightly golden then transfer to the lined tin. Fold over the baking parchment to enclose the fish and bake for 7 minutes. Remove from the oven, unwrap the fish and leave to cool.

5. Meanwhile, using your thumb and forefinger crush the potatoes into pieces about the same size as the olives. Using a fork or your fingers, flake the cooled fish onto a serving platter. Spoon the potatoes, olives and sliced white spring onions over the fish, then scatter the green spring onion strips and chilli on top. Drizzle the dressing over the salad and garnish with parsley.

FANTASTIC FORMAGGI

While I was in Trentino-Alto Adige filming this series, I had the good fortune of being able to tour the Dolomite Cheese Route (*la Strada dei Formaggi*), tasting all the amazing cheeses made there and watching artisan cheesemakers at work, using the same traditional methods as their ancestors many generations ago.

Cheese has been produced in Italy for thousands of years – sheep's cheese was known in Sicily in prehistoric times, and the art of cheesemaking was well established throughout the peninsula by the days of the Roman Empire. Indeed, wealthy Romans were so keen on the product they even installed a separate kitchen (*caseale*) in their villas for storing, aging and smoking cheese. By the 10th century Italy was the cheesemaking centre of Europe. Today there are between 450 and 600 different types of cheese made throughout Italy, with 75 per cent produced in the north – mainly in the dairy-rich Alpine areas and the Po Valley. Unlike in Britain, in Italy we always serve cheese before the *dolce* (dessert) as we like to end the meal on something sweet.

There are so many wonderful cheeses to choose from in northern Italy. Here are just some of my favourite varieties:

Asiago A cow's milk cheese (formerly made from sheep's milk) from Veneto and Trentino. Asiago pressato is young, smooth and mild, while mature Asiago d'allevo is sharper and more crumbly. Both are good for cooking.

Caprino A goat's cheese, usually with cow's milk added, produced mainly in the Alpine regions. Can be fresh (soft and creamy) or aged (saltier and more tangy).

Fontina Sweet, nutty and with a buttery texture, this semi-soft cow's milk cheese from Val d'Aosta is mainly used for cooking but is also a good table cheese.

Formaggio di fossa (pit-aged cheese) Made from cow's and sheep's milk, this matures for about 60 days and is then placed in a straw-lined, sealed pit to mature further. It is pungent and spicy with a crumbly texture.

Gorgonzola Produced in Lombardy since the 9th century, this semi-soft, blue-veined cow's milk cheese has a gutsy flavour. Good as a table cheese or for cooking.

Grana Padano Similar to Parmesan, but with a more delicate, less nutty flavour.

Mascarpone Originally from Lombardy but now made all over northern Italy, this is a soft cheese made from cream. Good for cooking.

Parmigiano-Reggiano (Parmesan) Originally from Emilia-Romagna, this crumbly, nutty cheese is aged longer than any other Italian cheese. It is usually used for grating but may be served with pears, walnuts and honey.

Pecorino The name given to any hard sheep's milk cheese made in Italy, this is one of the most ancient of all cheeses. It has a salty flavour and is good for grating but is sometimes eaten as a table cheese.

Provolone Originally from southern Italy, but now produced mainly in Lombardy, this is a semi-hard cheese for the table or cooking.

Ricotta Very light whey cheese made from milk that has been cooked twice (*ricotta* means 'recooked'). The best ricotta is made from sheep's milk rather than cow's milk.

Taleggio A semi-soft cheese from the Po Valley – mainly Lombardy but also Piedmont and Veneto – with a soft, melt-in-the-mouth texture and pungent aroma. Great for cooking.

MUSSELS COOKED IN WHITE WINE WITH CHERRY TOMATOES AND CHILLIES

Cozze alla marinara

SERVES 8

2kg live mussels
6 tablespoons extra
  virgin olive oil
4 garlic cloves, peeled
  and finely chopped
3 fresh, medium-hot
  red chillies, deseeded
  and finely sliced
1 large handful (about
  40g) of chopped fresh
  flat-leaf parsley
100ml dry white wine
600g fresh red cherry
  tomatoes, quartered
Salt and freshly ground
  black pepper

Mussels are eaten all over Italy – in soups, pasta sauces, or stuffed and baked. Steaming them in white wine, with tomatoes, garlic and fresh herbs – as in this recipe – is also popular. Quick to prepare, simple and nutritious, it is a wonderfully informal dish to share with family and friends. Serve with plenty of crusty bread to dunk in the sauce together with chilled white wine.

1. Scrub the mussels under cold running water. Rinse away grit and remove barnacles with a small, sharp knife. Remove the 'beards' by pulling the dark, stringy piece away from the mussels. Discard any open mussels or mussels with broken shells.

2. Heat the oil in a large saucepan. Add the mussels, cover and cook over a high heat for 2 minutes or until some of the mussels start to open. Reduce the heat slightly and stir in the garlic, chillies and parsley. Cover and cook for a further 2 minutes.

3. Remove the lid, pour in the wine and simmer for about 1 minute until it has evaporated. Add the tomatoes, season with salt and pepper and cook uncovered for a further 2 minutes. Discard any mussels that remain closed. Ladle into warm bowls and serve immediately.

Ribollita

SERVES 4

4 tablespoons olive oil
300g Italian pork sausages (optional)
2 small red onions, peeled and chopped
3 garlic cloves, peeled and chopped
2 carrots, peeled and chopped
3 celery sticks, chopped
1 potato, peeled and cut into 5mm cubes
Pinch of fennel seeds, crushed
1 bay leaf
Pinch of dried chilli flakes
2 fresh plum tomatoes, diced
1 x 400g tin of plum tomatoes
2 large handfuls of stale country-style bread, torn into chunks
700ml hot vegetable stock
1 x 400g tin of cannellini beans, rinsed and drained
300g kale, leaves and stalks finely sliced
6 tablespoons extra virgin olive oil
Sea salt and freshly ground black pepper

Each year in October a major cycling event known as *L'Eroica* takes place in Tuscany. The spirit is friendly and celebratory rather than competitive, it is open to anyone using a 'vintage' bike (pre-1980s) and many riders and volunteers wear historical costumes. The 'race' starts in Gaiole – a town in the wine-producing Chianti region – and ends in Siena. Along the route there are various 'aid stations', where the cyclists can 'refuel' on locally produced bread, salamis, cheeses and the classic Tuscan soup *ribollita* (which means 'reboiled', as traditionally it was made in large batches and reheated the next day). Thick, hearty and wholesome it is a meal in itself, particularly if you add the sausages (but they are not essential).

1. If using the sausages, heat 2 tablespoons of the olive oil in a large frying pan. Add the sausages and fry for about 12–15 minutes, turning frequently, until browned and cooked through. Set aside. When cool, cut into slices.

2. Heat the remaining 2 tablespoons of oil in a large saucepan over a medium heat. Add the onions, garlic, carrots, celery and potato, then the fennel, bay leaf and chilli flakes. Reduce the heat and cover, leaving the lid slightly ajar. Cook gently for 15–20 minutes or until softened but not brown, stirring occasionally.

3. Add the fresh and tinned tomatoes. Increase the heat and bring to a simmer. Meanwhile, put the bread in a medium bowl and pour over 200ml of the stock. Leave until the bread soaks up the stock (about 2 minutes).

4. Add the beans and the remaining stock to the pan and bring to the boil. Stir in the kale then the moistened bread. Reduce the heat and simmer for about 30 minutes.

5. Season with salt and pepper and add the extra virgin olive oil. Stir in the sausage, if using, heat through and then serve.

Zuppa di fagioli e lenticchie alla Piemontese

SERVES 4

100ml olive oil
2 large garlic cloves, crushed
1 large red onion, peeled and finely chopped
2 large carrots, peeled and finely chopped
3 celery sticks, finely chopped
1 large sprig of fresh rosemary
1 large sprig of fresh thyme
2 bay leaves
1 litre hot vegetable stock
1 x 400g tin of borlotti beans, rinsed and drained
1 x 400g tin of cannellini beans, rinsed and drained
1 x 400g tin of green lentils, rinsed and drained
Salt and freshly ground black pepper

When we were filming in the region of Piedmont we had this wholesome soup on countless occasions. Given the popularity of beans in Italy, it is hard to imagine that most kinds were unknown there until the 16th century, when they arrived from the New World. They were first cultivated in Veneto and spread all over northern and central Italy, where different varieties (including cannellini and borlotti beans) developed. Serve with focaccia.

1. Heat the oil in a large saucepan over a medium heat. Add the garlic and fry gently for 1 minute, stirring frequently. Add the onion, carrots, celery and the herbs and fry for 15 minutes or until softened, stirring occasionally.

2. Add the vegetable stock. Bring to the boil over a high heat then reduce the heat and simmer for 10 minutes.

3. Tip in the borlotti and cannellini beans and the lentils. Season with salt and pepper. Bring back to the boil and simmer for 3 minutes. Remove the herbs and ladle the soup into warm bowls.

FRESH PEA SOUP WITH EGG AND GRANA PADANO CHEESE

Zuppa di piselli freschi con uova e Grana Padano

SERVES 4

3 tablespoons olive oil
1 small onion, peeled and finely chopped
1 litre hot chicken or vegetable stock
500g fresh shelled peas
1 large egg
25g freshly grated Grana Padano cheese, plus extra to serve
Salt and freshly ground black pepper

Pea soups are popular in northern and central Italy, particularly in Veneto. This is a light, delicate, broth-based version with egg whisked in at the end to give a smooth, creamy texture and cheese for added flavour. Young, sweet tender peas are best, but if you can't find them use frozen peas instead and cook them for just 3 minutes.

1. Heat the oil in a medium saucepan over a medium heat. Add the onion and fry for 5–10 minutes, stirring occasionally.

2. Pour in the stock and bring to the boil over a high heat. Tip in the peas and bring back to the boil, then reduce the heat and simmer, uncovered, for 10–15 minutes or until they are tender but still have some texture. Season with salt and pepper. Remove the soup from the heat and leave to cool slightly (about 5 minutes).

3. Crack the egg into a small bowl and beat lightly with a fork. Add the Grana Padano and mix well. Pour the egg into the soup in a slow, steady stream, whisking rapidly as you pour. The egg will set in strands.

4. Ladle the soup into bowls. Sprinkle over extra Grana Padano and a grinding of black pepper and serve immediately.

SUMMER MINESTRONE

Minestrone estivo

SERVES 8

80ml olive oil
1 onion, peeled and
  finely chopped
2 large carrots, peeled
  and finely chopped
4 celery sticks, finely
  chopped
1 large sprig of fresh
  rosemary
1 bay leaf
250g baby new
  potatoes, scrubbed
  and halved
125g spring onions,
  finely sliced
300g baby carrots
300g baby courgettes,
  halved lengthways
  then cut into half
  moons, 1cm thick
200g fine green beans,
  trimmed and cut into
  2cm lengths
1.5 litres hot chicken
  or vegetable stock
200g fresh baby
  spinach leaves
3 tablespoons chopped
  fresh flat-leaf parsley
Salt and freshly ground
  black pepper

Minestrone is a classic Italian soup, but there is no fixed recipe and it varies according to availability of ingredients. This version contains a great mixture of summer vegetables and fresh herbs. If you like, add a teaspoon of pesto to each bowl and swirl it in – a Ligurian touch.

1. Heat the oil in a large saucepan over a medium heat. Add the onion, chopped carrots, half the celery, rosemary and bay leaf. Fry for 15 minutes, stirring occasionally. Season with salt and pepper.

2. Add the potatoes, spring onions, baby carrots and the remaining celery and fry for 5 minutes, stirring occasionally. Tip in the courgettes and green beans, season again and fry for 10 minutes, stirring occasionally.

3. Pour in the stock and bring to the boil. Reduce the heat, cover and simmer for 10 minutes. Stir in the spinach and parsley and simmer for 1 minute. Ladle the soup into warm bowls and serve immediately.

SEAFOOD SOUP WITH PEARL BARLEY

Zuppa di frutti di mare e orzo

SERVES 8

15 live clams
15 live mussels
100ml olive oil
2 onions, peeled and
  finely chopped
1 carrot, peeled and
  finely chopped
1 celery stick, finely
  chopped
1 fresh, medium-hot
  red chilli, deseeded
  and finely chopped
3 sprigs of fresh flat-
  leaf parsley
250g pearl barley,
  rinsed and drained
100ml dry white wine
2 litres hot fish stock
16 raw, peeled king
  prawns or
  langoustines,
  deveined and
  chopped into bite-
  sized pieces
Salt and freshly ground
  black pepper

Containing three different types of shellfish, this healthy and appetising soup is ideal for the seafood lover. The pearl barley gives substance and bite, and soaks up the flavour from the stock, while the chilli adds colour and zing. Serve with toasted ciabatta.

1. Soak the clams in cold salted water for 1 hour, drain well and scrub the shells under cold running water. Discard any open clams or clams with broken shells. Set aside. Scrub the mussels under cold running water. Rinse away the grit and remove barnacles with a small, sharp knife. Remove the 'beards' by pulling the dark, stringy piece away from the mussels. Discard any open mussels or mussels with broken shells. Set aside.

2. Heat the oil in a large pan over a medium heat. Add the onions, carrot, celery, chilli and parsley sprigs and fry gently for 10 minutes. Add the pearl barley and cook for 1 minute.

3. Increase the heat to high and pour in the wine. Cook for 2 minutes or until the liquid has almost evaporated, then add the stock and 500ml of water. Bring to the boil then reduce the heat and simmer gently for 40 minutes or until the barley is tender. Season with salt and pepper.

4. Remove a quarter of the soup and blitz until smooth using a hand-held blender, then return it to the pan. Add the clams, mussels and prawns or langoustines. Reduce the heat, cover and simmer for 3–5 minutes or until the mussels are open and the prawns or langoustines pink. Do not allow the soup to boil, or it will toughen the shellfish.

5. Ladle the soup into warm bowls, discarding any clams and mussels that remain closed. Serve immediately.

Brodo di manzo con uova in camicia e formaggio

SERVES 6

1kg–1.2kg beef bones

1 large onion, peeled and halved

1 leek, cut into large chunks

4 carrots, peeled (3 cut into large chunks, 1 sliced into rounds)

4 celery sticks (3 cut into large chunks, 1 diced)

2 bay leaves

1 teaspoon black peppercorns

1 x 750ml bottle of dry white wine

3 spring onions, finely chopped

6 eggs

2 tablespoons freshly grated Grana Padano cheese, plus extra to serve

Salt

Clear soups are very popular in Trentino-Alto Adige and often contain meat dumplings (*canederli*), strips of pancake or eggs, as in this recipe. This light, nourishing soup is perfect for when you want to curl up and be comforted, and although it may seem like a labour of love I promise it's worth it. Make the stock at least one day before you want to serve the soup.

1. Preheat the oven to 230°C/gas mark 8. Put the beef bones in a large roasting tin and roast for 30 minutes. Meanwhile, put the onion, leek, and carrot and celery chunks in a large, deep saucepan with the bay leaves and peppercorns. Pour in the wine and 5 litres of cold water. Bring to the boil over a high heat. Skim off any froth from the surface using a slotted spoon.

2. Transfer the bones to the pan. Reduce the heat, cover and simmer gently for 2½ hours with the lid on, then remove the lid and cook for a further 2 hours. Top up with extra water if you need to. Remove and discard the bones.

3. Strain the broth through a fine sieve into another large pan and discard the vegetables. Season the broth with salt. Leave to cool then cover the pan with cling film and refrigerate overnight.

4. Remove the cling film and scoop off and discard the solidified fat on the surface. Return the broth to a medium heat and bring to the boil. Add the spring onions, carrot rounds and diced celery. Reduce the heat and simmer for 3–5 minutes. Preheat the grill for about 5 minutes on its highest setting.

5. In a separate pan, poach the eggs gently over a low heat for about 3 minutes (you will need to poach in batches, 1 or 2 eggs at a time). Remove using a slotted spoon and transfer to kitchen paper to drain.

6. Ladle the broth into warm bowls. Carefully slide a poached egg on top and sprinkle over the Grana Padano. Transfer the bowls to the grill and cook for 3 minutes or until the cheese is golden and bubbling. Sprinkle extra cheese over the top and serve immediately.

No Italian cookbook would be complete without a section devoted to pasta – it is the most popular first course in Italy, with each region having its own specialities (see page 54). Always cook pasta in a large pan with 5 litres of boiling water and 2 tablespoons of salt for 500g of pasta. Never overcook it – it must have the al dente bite.

PASTA

Fettuccine allo zafferano fatte in casa

**SERVES 4-6
(MAKES ABOUT
500G)**

350g '00' grade pasta
  flour, plus extra for
  dusting
3 large eggs
0.75g saffron powder
½ teaspoon fine salt
1 tablespoon extra
  virgin olive oil

When I visited Lake Como I met a cook called Francesca, who showed me how to make fresh egg fettuccine flavoured with saffron – a classic dish that dates back to the Renaissance. It was delicious, so here is the recipe for you to try. It goes beautifully with a rich meat sauce (see page 48).

1. Dust a large tray with flour and set aside. In a medium bowl, lightly beat the eggs with the saffron. Place the flour and salt in a large bowl. Make a well in the centre and add the beaten eggs and oil. Using the handle of a wooden spoon, gradually mix the flour into the liquid. Once the texture is crumbly, resembling breadcrumbs, turn out the mixture onto a well-floured work surface.

2. Knead the mixture until you have a soft, smooth dough (this should take about 8–10 minutes). The method is the same as for bread: hold the dough in one hand while you fold, push down and stretch the dough away from you with the other hand. Rotate the dough as you go. Shape the dough into a ball, wrap in cling film and refrigerate for 30 minutes.

3. Dust a rolling pin, the dough and the work surface again with flour to prevent sticking. Flatten the dough with the palm of your hand, then place the rolling pin across one end of the dough and roll it towards the centre. Continue to roll the pin backwards and forwards. Rotate the dough and repeat several times. When the dough has spread out evenly and is so thinly rolled that you can see your hands through it, it's ready.

4. Loosely roll up the sheet of dough to form a flat roll, like a flattened cigar, from one edge to the centre, then repeat from the other edge to the centre. Dust the pasta with flour.

5. Using a long knife, cut across the pasta roll to make 5mm-wide strips. Slide the knife beneath the rolled pasta sheet, lining up the edge of the knife with the centre of the folds. Gently lift the knife so that the pasta ribbons fall down on each side. Toss the fettuccine with a little more flour, place on the floured tray and cover with cling film until you are ready to cook (no more than 3 hours).

6. Cook the fettuccine in a large pan of boiling, salted water for about 3 minutes or until al dente. Drain thoroughly and serve with a sauce of your choice.

SAFFRON FETTUCCINE WITH A RICH MEAT SAUCE

Fettuccine allo zafferano con ragù

SERVES 6

5 tablespoons olive oil
1 red onion, peeled
  and finely chopped
1 large carrot, peeled
  and finely chopped
2 celery sticks, finely
  chopped
2 tablespoons chopped
  fresh rosemary
500g minced beef
500g minced lamb
300ml full-bodied
  red wine
3 x 400g tins of
  chopped tomatoes
200ml hot beef stock
2 tablespoons tomato
  purée
500g home-made
  saffron fettuccine
  (see page 47)
Salt and freshly ground
  black pepper

The rich meat pasta sauces of northern Italy usually contain two or more different kinds of minced or finely chopped meat. Near Turin they tend to combine beef and lamb, which I initially thought was a little strange until I tried it and found the textures and flavours really complemented each other. Make sure you cook the sauce for the full cooking time as a good ragù must be cooked very slowly for at least two hours.

1. Heat the oil in a large, heavy-based saucepan or flameproof casserole over a medium heat. Add the onion, carrot, celery and rosemary and fry gently for 8–10 minutes, stirring frequently. Add the beef and lamb and fry for 8 minutes or until browned, stirring continuously.

2. Pour in the wine and simmer for about 2 minutes. Add the tomatoes, stock and tomato purée and season with salt and pepper. Reduce the heat and cook, uncovered, for at least 2 hours, stirring occasionally. Check for seasoning and set aside.

3. Cook the fettuccine in a large pan of boiling, salted water for about 3 minutes or until al dente. Drain the pasta thoroughly and tip it back into the same pan.

4. Pour over the sauce and stir for 30 seconds to allow all the flavours to combine. Serve immediately.

Linguine con capesante e pesto di prezzemolo

SERVES 4

2 tablespoons salted
  butter
1 tablespoon olive oil
250g small scallops,
  trimmed
Grated zest of 1
  unwaxed lemon
500g dried linguine
Salt and freshly
  ground black pepper

For the pesto
60g fresh flat-leaf
  parsley leaves
60g pine nuts
2 tablespoons capers,
  drained
1 garlic clove, peeled
130ml extra virgin
  olive oil

In the north of Italy, on the Adriatic coast, you'll find lots of dishes that feature scallops. I particularly like this pasta recipe because it's so quick and I love the delicate flavours and textures. If you're not a fan of scallops use peeled prawns instead. Please do not be tempted to sprinkle Parmesan or other cheese on top as it will overwhelm the flavour of the scallops.

1. Heat the butter and oil in a large frying pan over a high heat. Add the scallops and fry for 1 minute each side or until golden. Set aside.

2. To make the pesto, place the parsley, pine nuts, capers and garlic in a food processor and blitz until smooth. With the blades turning, add the oil gradually in a thin, steady stream until the sauce thickens and emulsifies.

3. Transfer the pesto to a large bowl. Carefully stir in the scallops and lemon zest and season with salt and pepper. Set aside.

4. Cook the linguine in a large pan of boiling, salted water until al dente. Drain the pasta thoroughly and tip it into the bowl with the scallops and pesto. Gently stir for 30 seconds to combine. Serve immediately.

Pasta e fagioli

SERVES 4

4 tablespoons olive oil
150g diced smoked
  pancetta
3 garlic cloves, peeled
  and sliced
2 tablespoons chopped
  fresh rosemary
½ teaspoon dried chilli
  flakes
2 x 400g tins of
  borlotti beans, rinsed
  and drained
1 x 400g tin of
  cannellini beans,
  rinsed and drained
1 x 400g tin of
  chickpeas, rinsed
  and drained
1.5 litres hot vegetable
  stock
300g dried gomiti
  (elbow) pasta
20 fresh red cherry
  tomatoes, halved
60g freshly grated
  Grana Padano cheese
Salt

This is a fantastic recipe for when you need a 'quick-fix' supper – most of the ingredients are dried or tinned, so it's likely you'll have them in your storecupboard, and very little chopping or other preparation is required. Beans and chickpeas are an inexpensive, low-fat source of protein, fibre and vitamins, so this dish is both healthy and economical. For vegetarians, simply omit the pancetta and use a rennet-free cheese.

1. Heat the oil in a large saucepan over a medium heat. Fry the pancetta for 6 minutes, stirring occasionally. Add the garlic, rosemary and chilli flakes and fry for 2 minutes. Stir in the borlotti and cannellini beans and the chickpeas and cook for 2 minutes.

2. Pour in the stock, reduce the heat and simmer gently for 30 minutes with the lid half on, stirring occasionally.

3. Add the pasta and cook it in the liquid for about 8 minutes, uncovered, or until al dente. (If the sauce is reducing too quickly, add a cup of hot water.)

4. Remove from the heat, leave to rest for 2 minutes then stir in the tomatoes and Grana Padano. Taste for seasoning. Serve immediately.

A PASSION FOR PASTA

I can't imagine life without pasta. When I was growing up in Naples we ate it nearly every day and my family and I still enjoy it several times a week. No one knows for certain where pasta originated. People used to think Marco Polo brought it to Venice from China in the 13th century, but it is more likely to have been introduced by the Arabs to Sicily. Either way, by the 15th century pasta was certainly enjoyed in southern and central Italy, while rice was the staple food of northern Italians. In fact, pasta has only really taken off in many regions of northern Italy – including Piedmont, Liguria and Lombardy – in the last century. Today it is a key part of the northern Italian diet, both dried (*pasta secca*) and fresh (*pasta fresca*), and each region has its own special pasta shapes and sauces. On the coast you'll find amazing seafood sauces, in the mountains rich meaty ragùs – often using boar or rabbit – and in central Italy hearty vegetable sauces are common, sometimes using potatoes or beans. You really could quite easily enjoy a different pasta dish every day of the year.

There are over 650 different pasta shapes in Italy. Here are just a few.

Bigoli Long, thick spaghetti-like pasta from Veneto made with wholewheat or buckwheat flour, butter and duck eggs.

Gigli Meaning 'lily', and also known as campanelle ('little bells'), this pasta from Tuscany is shaped like a bell-shaped flower with a ruffled edge.

Gomiti Sometimes referred to as elbow pasta, this is a short, curved macaroni.

Maccheroni Short, hollow-tubed pasta. Confusingly, in southern Italy the term is often used to refer to all pasta.

Pizzoccheri Buckwheat pasta produced in Lombardy that resembles short tagliatelle, but is dark or grey-brown and freckled.

Spaghetti alla chitarra A speciality of Abruzzo, this pasta is made using a *chitarra* ('guitar') – a traditional wooden frame with sharp metal cutting wires stretched across, through which rolled-out pasta dough is pressed with a rolling pin. It resembles spaghetti but is square in cross-section.

Strozzapreti Meaning 'priest-strangler' in Italian, and sometimes also known as strangozzi, this is short twisted pasta from Tuscany and Umbria.

Tagliatelle Also known as fettuccine or taglierini, tagliatelle are long, flat noodles about 1cm wide. In some areas of northern Italy they are made with chestnut flour and are called Tagliatelle alle castagne.

Trofie Small, short, rolled pasta originally from Liguria.

Stuffed pasta There are many forms of filled pasta in northern Italy, all of which are very similar but have different names: agnolotti (Piedmont); ravioli (Tuscany); cappelletti, tortelli, tortellini and tortelloni (Emilia-Romagna); casonsei and casoncelli (Lombardy); cjalsons (Friuli) and pansotti (Liguria). They can be round, half-moon shaped, square or hat-shaped and are filled with a meat mixture or with cheese, eggs, herbs or seasonal vegetables – *zucca* (pumpkin), spinach and beets make particularly popular fillings.

FRESH PAPPARDELLE TOSSED IN BUTTER WITH FRESH TRUFFLE SHAVINGS

Pappardelle al burro e tartufo

SERVES 4

400g fresh pappardelle
100g salted butter
1 small fresh black
  summer truffle
60g freshly grated
  Parmesan cheese
Salt and white pepper

When we were filming in Piedmont we visited the Truffle Festival in Alba. The town is famous for its white truffles, which are available only two months of the year and are the world's most expensive food by weight. Black summer truffles, which I've used for this recipe, are more widely available, less costly, and more versatile. Buried in the soil around trees, truffles are hard to find, so truffle hunters (*trifolau*) use a specially trained dog to sniff them out. Traditionally, female pigs were used, but this has been banned in Italy since the 1980s because they damaged the truffles.

1. Cook the pappardelle in a large pan of boiling, salted water until al dente. Meanwhile, melt the butter slowly in a small saucepan over a low heat. Add a large pinch of pepper. Set aside and keep warm.

2. Drain the pasta thoroughly and tip it back into the same pan. Pour over the melted butter, season with salt and stir for 30 seconds to combine.

3. Divide the pappardelle between 4 plates or bowls. Shave over the fresh truffle using the coarse side of a grater and sprinkle over the Parmesan. Serve immediately.

Conchigliette al guanciale, patate e pomodori

SERVES 4

6 tablespoons extra virgin olive oil

1 large red onion, peeled and finely chopped

250g guanciale, cut into 1cm cubes

1 large carrot, peeled and cut into 1cm cubes

400g floury potatoes (e.g. Maris Piper or King Edward), peeled and cut into 2cm cubes

1.8 litres hot vegetable stock

1 x 400g tin of chopped tomatoes

300g dried conchigliette (small pasta shells)

80g freshly grated Parmesan cheese

Salt and freshly ground black pepper

This is the ultimate comfort food and a great winter dish to share with family and friends. Guanciale is pig's cheek that has been rubbed with salt, black pepper, sugar and thyme, then cured for three months. It is a delicacy from central Italy – particularly Umbria and Lazio – and is used in classic Roman pasta sauces such as amatriciana and carbonara. Smoked pancetta or bacon are good substitutes, although they have a milder flavour.

1. Heat the oil in a large saucepan over a medium heat. Add the onion and guanciale and fry for 5 minutes, stirring occasionally. Tip in the carrot and potatoes and fry for 2 minutes.

2. Pour in the stock and bring to the boil over a high heat. Reduce the heat and simmer gently for about 25 minutes (uncovered). Tip in the tomatoes and season with salt and pepper.

3. Add the conchigliette and cook over a low heat for about 8 minutes or until al dente, stirring occasionally. Remove from the heat, stir in the Parmesan and serve immediately.

QUICK FRESH EGG TAGLIATELLE IN A CHEESY TOMATO SAUCE WITH SPECK

Tagliatelle veloci con speck e formaggio

SERVES 2

4 tablespoons olive oil
80g speck, finely sliced
1 garlic clove, peeled
  and sliced
1 x 400g tin of chopped
  tomatoes
Large handful (about
  40g) of fresh basil,
  shredded, plus extra
  leaves to garnish
5 fresh lasagne sheets
300g freshly grated
  caciotta al timo
  cheese

When I was in Trentino-Alto Adige I visited a farm run by a delightful artisan cheesemaker called Graziano. Together we milked his cows and he showed me how to make the traditional caciotta al timo cheese, which is flavoured with thyme. As a thank you I created this pasta dish for him, using locally sourced speck – a kind of smoked prosciutto. Getting hold of caciotta al timo can be tricky, but Cheddar, fontina and grated mozzarella will work well too. Smoked pancetta is a good substitute for speck.

1. Heat 3 tablespoons of the oil in a frying pan over a high heat. Add the speck and fry for 5–6 minutes or until crisp. Stir in the garlic and fry for 2–3 minutes or until golden then add the tomatoes and bring to the boil. Reduce the heat, stir in the basil and add the remaining tablespoon of oil. Simmer for 5–7 minutes.

2. Meanwhile, slice the lasagne sheets lengthways into strips about 1cm wide. Cook in a large pan of boiling, salted water until al dente.

3. Take the sauce off the heat and stir in half the cheese. Remove the pasta from the water using tongs or a spaghetti spoon and put directly into the sauce without draining. Toss together to coat the pasta.

4. Divide the pasta between 2 warm plates or bowls, sprinkle over the remaining cheese and garnish with basil leaves.

Rigatoni al sugo di cinghiale

SERVES 4

4 tablespoons olive oil
500g wild boar for
  stewing, trimmed and
  cut into 5cm cubes
1 red onion, peeled and
  chopped
1 large carrot, peeled
  and finely chopped
1 celery stick, finely
  chopped
150g diced smoked
  pancetta
300ml full-bodied
  red wine
1 x 400g tin of
  chopped tomatoes
100ml hot beef stock
4 tablespoons tomato
  purée
½ teaspoon fennel
  seeds
500g dried rigatoni
80g freshly grated
  Parmesan cheese
Salt and freshly ground
  black pepper

Wild boar were introduced to Italy from central Europe in the 1950s by hunters, and since then numbers have soared. In Tuscany, where they are most numerous (and cause damage to crops, vineyards and livestock), they are a local delicacy. In autumn and winter you'll find wild boar on the menu in most good Tuscan restaurants – like this delicious dish that I ordered when I last visited the region. Wild boar is richer and leaner than pork, but if you can't find boar, shoulder of pork is a good substitute.

1. Heat the oil in a medium, heavy-based saucepan or flameproof casserole over a medium to high heat. When hot, fry the wild boar in 2 batches until well browned on all sides. Remove the meat with a slotted spoon and transfer to a large bowl.

2. Reduce the heat to medium. Add the onion, carrot, celery and pancetta and fry gently for 8–10 minutes, stirring frequently. Increase the heat, pour in the wine and simmer until reduced by half. Add the tomatoes, stock and tomato purée and bring to the boil.

3. Return the meat to the pan with any juices. Bring to the boil then reduce the heat, cover and simmer gently for 1 hour, stirring occasionally. Add the fennel seeds, re-cover and cook for 1 further hour. Season with salt and pepper.

4. Cook the rigatoni in a large pan of boiling, salted water until al dente. Drain the pasta thoroughly and tip it back into the same pan. Pour over the sauce and stir for 30 seconds to combine.

5. Divide the rigatoni between 6 warmed bowls or plates. Sprinkle over the Parmesan and serve immediately.

SPAGHETTI ALLA CHITARRA WITH FRESH TOMATOES, GARLIC, CHILLI AND ROCKET

Spaghetti alla chitarra con pomodori freschi, aglio, peperoncino e rucola

SERVES 4

2 garlic cloves, peeled
  and sliced
3 tablespoons olive oil,
  plus extra for drizzling
2 or 3 pinches of dried
  chilli flakes
300g fresh red
  cherry or baby plum
  tomatoes, halved
120ml dry white wine
500g dried spaghetti
  alla chitarra
Handful (about 40g)
  of rocket leaves
Salt

When I was in Pescara – the main city in the Abruzzo region – I spent the morning with Giovanni Minicucci, the founder of the pasta shop Chitarra Antica, making spaghetti alla chitarra in the traditional way (see page 54). I then rustled up a quick fresh tomato and chilli pasta sauce – the type that every Italian makes at home. So simple yet so delicious. If you can't find spaghetti alla chitarra use any good-quality spaghetti for this dish.

1. Put the garlic in a large cold frying pan. Add the oil and place the pan over a medium heat. As soon as the garlic begins to brown add the chilli flakes.

2. Add the tomatoes and cook for 2 minutes, stirring continuously, until slightly softened. Season with salt. Increase the heat, pour in the wine and simmer for about 2 minutes until it has evaporated. Reduce the heat and simmer gently for 4–5 minutes.

3. Cook the pasta in a large pan of boiling, salted water until al dente. Remove the pasta from the water using tongs or a spaghetti spoon and put it directly in the pan with the tomatoes without draining. Stir thoroughly to combine. Drizzle with a little extra oil, add the rocket and toss together. Serve immediately.

PASTA BAKE WITH SMOKED SALMON, FONTINA AND PEAS

Pennette gratinate al salmone affumicato, fontina e piselli

SERVES 4

300g dried pennette
  rigate
150g smoked salmon,
  cut into thin strips
150g frozen peas,
  defrosted
3 tablespoons snipped
  fresh chives
150g fontina cheese,
  rind removed and cut
  into small pieces
Butter for greasing

For the béchamel
50g salted butter
50g plain flour
500ml full-fat milk
1 pinch of freshly
  grated nutmeg
½ teaspoon smoked
  sweet paprika
Salt and white pepper

This is a fantastic way to use smoked salmon, and many people who don't generally like fish – such as my wife – love this recipe. If the béchamel and pasta are hot you can just pop the dish under the grill until the cheese melts, as I've done here. If you want to make it ahead, prepare up to the end of step 4 then reheat the dish in a preheated oven (200°C/gas mark 6) for 20–25 minutes. If you prefer, use smoked trout instead of salmon.

1. First make the béchamel sauce. Melt the butter in a medium saucepan over a medium heat until foaming. Add the flour and cook for 1–2 minutes or until pale golden, stirring continuously.

2. Start adding the milk a little at a time, whisking constantly and waiting for it to be incorporated before adding more. Bring to the boil then reduce the heat and simmer gently for 5–10 minutes, whisking occasionally, until thickened and smooth. Add the nutmeg and paprika and season with salt and pepper. Remove from the heat and set aside to cool slightly.

3. Cook the pennette in a large pan of boiling, salted water until al dente. Drain thoroughly and tip it into a large bowl. Add the smoked salmon, peas and chives, and half each of the fontina and the béchamel. Stir to combine. Preheat the grill to medium.

4. Grease a round baking dish, 25cm diameter. Tip in the pasta mixture, cover with the remaining béchamel and scatter over the remaining fontina.

5. Place the dish under the grill and cook for 5 minutes or until golden. Leave to rest for about 5 minutes, then serve.

Risotto is so versatile and easy to make. It's a great one-pot dish and you can have a meal on the table within 30–40 minutes. OK, you do have to stay by your pan, stirring – but with a glass of wine in hand this can be a pleasure rather than a chore. Make sure you use Italian risotto rice, as its high starch content creates a creamy texture.

RISOTTO

ASPARAGUS, BROAD BEAN, PEA AND   73
LEEK RISOTTO

Risotto primavera alle verdure di stagione

SERVES 6

500g fine asparagus
   spears
200g leeks
200g podded fresh
   or frozen young
   broad beans,
   defrosted
250g shelled fresh
   or frozen peas,
   defrosted
100ml olive oil
100g salted butter
400g Arborio,
   Carnaroli or Vialone
   Nano rice
150ml dry white wine
3 tablespoons chopped
   fresh flat-leaf parsley
60g freshly grated
   Grana Padano
   cheese, plus extra
   to serve
Salt and freshly ground
   black pepper

For me, this wonderful risotto signals the end of spring and the start of summer. If using older beans it's best to remove their skins after boiling as they can be tough. You can use frozen broad beans and peas if you prefer.

1. Cut the woody ends from the asparagus and the tough green parts from the leeks. Reserve the trimmings for the stock. Remove the tips from the asparagus and set aside. Finely chop the asparagus stalks and the leeks and set aside.

2. To make the stock, put 1.5 litres of water in a medium saucepan with 1½ teaspoons salt and bring to the boil. If using fresh broad beans and peas, tip them into the water and cook for 3 minutes then remove with a slotted spoon and set aside (omit this step if using frozen peas and beans). Add the trimmings from the asparagus and leeks to the pan, bring back to the boil, then reduce the heat and simmer over a very low heat for 20–30 minutes. Discard the trimmings and keep the stock warm over a very low heat.

3. Bring a small saucepan of salted water to the boil. Add the asparagus tips, cook for 2 minutes then drain well and keep warm.

4. Heat the oil and butter in a large saucepan over a medium heat. Add the chopped leeks and asparagus stalks and fry for 10 minutes. Add the rice and stir constantly for 2 minutes or until the grains are coated and shiny. Pour in the wine and simmer for about 1 minute until it has evaporated.

5. Add 2 ladlesful of the stock, bring to a simmer and stir until it is absorbed. Continue adding the rest of the stock in the same way, stirring and waiting for it to be absorbed before adding more, until the rice is cooked but still has a slight bite. It should take about 16–18 minutes. You may not need to use all the stock. Stir in the broad beans and peas (cooked fresh or frozen defrosted) and parsley.

6. Remove the pan from the heat and add the Grana Padano, stirring for about 30 seconds until creamy. Season with salt and pepper. To serve, garnish with the reserved asparagus tips and sprinkle over extra cheese.

74

CHICORY AND PANCETTA RISOTTO WITH RED WINE

Risotto al vino rosso, pancetta e cicoria

SERVES 6

4 tablespoons olive oil
2 shallots, peeled and finely sliced
200g diced smoked pancetta
400g Arborio, Carnaroli or Vialone Nano rice
300g chicory, white part finely sliced and green tips left whole
500ml dry, fruity red wine (preferably Barolo)
50g salted butter
70g freshly grated Grana Padano cheese

For the stock
1 onion, peeled and halved
1 carrot, peeled and roughly chopped
1 celery stick, roughly chopped
Salt and freshly ground black pepper

This is a sophisticated risotto with a rich flavour and beautiful deep colour. I've used Barolo – a dry, aromatic, fruity wine from Piedmont – but you can use any good-quality red. To intensify the colour replace the chicory with radicchio, which is sometimes called 'red chicory' and is highly prized in rice dishes in Veneto. They taste similar, but chicory has a slightly stronger flavour than radicchio. Here I have given instructions for making vegetable stock, but if you're short of time use a stock cube.

1. To make the stock, put 1 litre of cold water in a medium saucepan with the onion, carrot and celery, 1 teaspoon of salt and some pepper. Bring to the boil then reduce the heat to low, cover and simmer for 1–1½ hours. Discard the vegetables and keep warm over a very low heat.

2. Meanwhile, heat the oil in a large saucepan over a medium heat. Add the shallots and fry for 5 minutes then add the pancetta and cook for 5 minutes, stirring occasionally. Tip in the rice and stir constantly for 2 minutes or until the grains are coated and shiny.

3. Add the sliced chicory and stir for 1 minute or until it starts to wilt. Gradually add half the wine, stirring constantly, until it is absorbed.

4. Add 2 ladlesful of the stock. Bring to a simmer and stir until it is absorbed. Continue adding the rest of the stock in the same way, stirring and waiting for it to be absorbed before adding more. After about 12 minutes add the remaining wine a little at a time, stirring constantly (it should take about 5 minutes). Stir in the chicory tips and cook for about 1 minute or until wilted.

5. Remove the pan from the heat and add the butter and half the Grana Padano, stirring for about 30 seconds until creamy. Season with salt and pepper. Sprinkle over the remaining cheese and serve immediately.

COURGETTE, PEA AND WALNUT RISOTTO

Risotto con fiori di zucchine, piselli e noci

SERVES 4

6 baby courgettes with the flower
6 tablespoons olive oil
2 shallots, peeled and finely sliced
300g Arborio, Carnaroli or Vialone Nano rice
200ml dry white wine
300g frozen peas, defrosted
1.3 litres hot vegetable stock (see page 74, step 1)
50g walnuts, roughly chopped
150ml double cream
50g salted butter
70g freshly grated Parmesan cheese
Salt and white pepper

For this seasonal summer risotto try to find the flavoursome small, young courgettes with a flower attached so you can use the petals in the dish. I like to garnish this risotto with a deep-fried courgette flower (see page 21). It's extra work but looks beautiful and tastes delicious.

1. First prepare the courgettes. Using your fingers, carefully part the flower petals and remove and discard the stamens. Thinly shred the petals and finely slice the courgettes. Set aside.

2. Heat the oil in a medium saucepan over a medium heat. Add the shallots and fry for 5 minutes, stirring occasionally. Add the rice and stir constantly for 2 minutes or until the grains are coated and shiny.

3. Pour in the wine and simmer for about 2 minutes until it has evaporated. Add half the peas then 2 ladlesful of stock. Bring to a simmer and stir until all the stock is absorbed. Continue adding the rest of the stock in the same way, stirring and waiting for it to be absorbed before adding more, until the rice is cooked but still has a slight bite. It should take about 16–18 minutes. You may not need to use all the stock.

4. Add the remaining peas, courgettes and walnuts and cook for about 2 minutes, stirring. Remove the pan from the heat and add the cream, butter and Parmesan, stirring for about 30 seconds. Season with some salt and pepper if needed. Garnish with a deep-fried courgette flower (if desired) and serve immediately.

Risotto alla Valdostana con pesto rosso

SERVES 4

100g salted butter
100ml olive oil
250g leeks, finely
  chopped
3 sprigs of fresh thyme
400g Carnaroli or
  Vialone Nano rice
150ml dry white wine
1 litre hot chicken
  stock
200g fontina cheese,
  rind removed and
  roughly chopped
150g good-quality,
  shop-bought red
  pesto

Fontina cheese – made in the Val d'Aosta in the western Alps since medieval times – is rich and creamy and has a nutty flavour. It also melts beautifully so is perfect for cooking and is often used in cheese fondues. If you can't get fontina, you can use Gorgonzola or any other soft blue cheese for this recipe. The red pesto stirred in at the end adds piquancy and colour.

1. Heat the butter and oil in a large saucepan over a medium heat. Add the leeks and thyme and fry for 5 minutes, stirring occasionally.

2. Add the rice and stir constantly for 2 minutes or until the grains are coated and shiny. Pour over the wine and simmer for about 1 minute, stirring, until it has evaporated.

3. Add 2 ladlesful of stock. Bring to a simmer and stir until all the stock is absorbed. Continue adding the rest of the stock in the same way, stirring and waiting for it to be absorbed before adding more, until the rice is cooked but still has a slight bite. It should take about 16–18 minutes. You may not need to use all the stock.

4. Remove the pan from the heat and add the fontina and red pesto, stirring for about 30 seconds until the cheese has melted. Serve immediately.

DUCK RISOTTO WITH MUSHROOMS AND CHERRY TOMATOES

Risotto all'anatra con funghi e pomodorini

SERVES 4

6 tablespoons olive oil
2 garlic cloves, peeled
200g chestnut
  mushrooms, sliced
2 shallots, peeled and
  finely sliced
3 sprigs of fresh
  thyme
2 duck breasts (about
  400g total), skinned
  and cut into 1cm
  cubes
400g Arborio,
  Carnaroli or Vialone
  Nano rice
200ml dry white wine
1 litre hot vegetable
  stock (see page 74,
  step 1)
20 fresh red cherry
  tomatoes, quartered
2 tablespoons
  chopped fresh flat-
  leaf parsley
70g salted butter
70g freshly grated
  Grana Padano cheese,
  plus extra to serve
Salt and freshly ground
  black pepper

Duck is widely bred all over northern Italy and has become increasingly popular in recent years. There are also many species of wild duck, particularly in the Po Delta in Veneto. The Po Valley is also where Italy's unique risotto rice is cultivated – mainly on the Lombardy plain and in Piedmont – so a duck risotto is the ultimate Po Valley dish!

1. Heat 2 tablespoons of the oil in a large frying pan over a medium heat. Add 1 garlic clove, fry for 2 minutes then discard. Increase the heat, add the mushrooms and cook for 5 minutes, stirring occasionally. Set aside.

2. Heat the remaining 4 tablespoons of oil in a medium saucepan over a medium heat. Add the remaining garlic clove, fry for 2 minutes then discard. Add the shallots and thyme and fry for 5 minutes, stirring, until softened but not browned.

3. Tip in the duck and fry for 3–5 minutes or until browned on all sides. Add the rice and stir constantly for 2 minutes or until the grains are coated and shiny. Pour in the wine and simmer for about 1 minute until it has evaporated. Stir in half the mushrooms.

4. Add 2 ladlesful of stock, bring to a simmer and stir until it is absorbed. Continue adding the rest of the stock in the same way, stirring and waiting for it to be absorbed before adding more, until the rice is cooked but still has a slight bite. It should take about 16–18 minutes. You may not need to use all the stock.

5. Stir in the tomatoes, parsley and remaining mushrooms. Remove the pan from the heat and add the butter and Grana Padano, stirring for about 30 seconds until creamy. Season with salt and pepper, sprinkle over extra cheese and serve immediately.

Risotto al salmone affumicato, asparagi e limone

SERVES 4

450g fine asparagus spears, woody ends removed

1 onion, peeled and halved

1 carrot, peeled and roughly chopped

1 celery stick, peeled and roughly chopped

6 tablespoons olive oil

4 shallots, finely sliced

2 bay leaves

300g Arborio, Carnaroli or Vialone Nano rice

400g smoked salmon, roughly chopped

Grated zest and juice of 1 unwaxed lemon

300ml dry white wine

50g salted butter

3 tablespoons snipped fresh chives

Salt and white pepper

Asparagus and smoked salmon are a classic combination, and although smoked salmon isn't traditional in Italy it's very popular and often found in restaurants. This risotto is perfect for midweek entertaining as it's impressive yet quick to prepare. Serve with a glass of chilled Pinot Grigio.

1. First make the stock. Put 1.3 litres of cold water and 1 teaspoon of salt in a medium saucepan and bring to the boil. Add the asparagus and cook for 2 minutes. Remove the asparagus using a slotted spoon and plunge it into a bowl of very cold water. Drain then cut into 1.5cm lengths.

2. Add the onion, carrot, celery and some pepper to the asparagus water and bring to the boil. Reduce the heat to low, cover and simmer for 30 minutes. Discard the vegetables and keep warm over a very low heat.

3. Meanwhile, heat the oil in a medium saucepan over a medium heat. Add the shallots and bay leaves and fry for 5 minutes, stirring occasionally. Discard the bay leaves. Add the rice and stir constantly for 2 minutes or until the grains are coated and shiny.

4. Add half each of the asparagus and smoked salmon, and stir in the lemon zest. Pour over the wine and lemon juice and simmer for about 2 minutes or until the liquid has evaporated.

5. Add 2 ladlesful of stock. Bring to a simmer and stir until it is absorbed. Add the rest of the stock in the same way, stirring and waiting for it to be absorbed before adding more, until the rice is cooked but still has a slight bite. It should take about 16–18 minutes. You may not need to use all the stock.

6. Stir in the remaining asparagus. Remove the pan from the heat and add the remaining smoked salmon, butter and chives, stirring for about 30 seconds until creamy. Season with some salt and pepper. Serve immediately.

SEAFOOD RISOTTO WITH GARLIC AND A HINT OF CHILLI

Risotto ai frutti di mare con aglio e peperoncino

SERVES 4

500g live clams
500g live mussels
300g raw peeled
  prawns, deveined
300ml dry white wine
4 tablespoons chopped
  fresh flat-leaf parsley
4 garlic cloves (2
  crushed and 2 finely
  chopped)
1 litre hot fish stock
4 tablespoons olive oil
1 teaspoon dried chilli
  flakes
300g Arborio,
  Carnaroli or Vialone
  Nano rice
Salt and white pepper

Risotto ai frutti di mare **is a classic northern Italian dish and some recipes contain four or five different types of seafood. Here I've added a little chilli for extra kick. Please don't add cheese as it 'fights' with the seafood.**

1. Prepare the clams and mussels (see page 40, step 1). Chop the prawns into bite-sized pieces, reserving a few for garnish, and set aside.

2. Put the clams and mussels in a large saucepan with 200ml of the wine, half the parsley, the crushed garlic and ½ teaspoon of salt. Bring to the boil, cover and simmer for 3 minutes or until the shellfish has just opened then strain, reserving the cooking liquid. Remove most of the clams and mussels from their shells, reserving a few in their shells to garnish. Set aside. Strain the cooking liquid into a small pan and add the stock. Bring to the boil, reduce the heat and simmer gently until needed.

3. Heat the oil in a medium saucepan over a medium heat. Add the chopped garlic and chilli flakes and fry for about 1 minute. Add the rice and stir constantly for 2 minutes or until the grains are coated and shiny. Pour in the remaining wine and simmer for about 1 minute until it has evaporated.

4. Add 2 ladlesful of stock. Bring to a simmer and stir until it is absorbed. Continue adding the rest of the stock in the same way, stirring and waiting for it to be absorbed before adding more.

5. After 12 minutes stir in the chopped prawns, the shelled clams and mussels and the remaining parsley. Season with salt if needed. Continue to stir for a further 5 minutes or until the rice is cooked but still has a slight bite.

6. Remove the pan from the heat and leave to rest, covered, for 2 minutes. Garnish with the reserved clams, mussels and prawns then serve.

Pomodori alla Milanese

SERVES 6

Large pinch of saffron
  threads
300g Arborio, Carnaroli
  or Vialone Nano rice
12 fresh ripe beef
  tomatoes
4 tablespoons olive oil,
  plus extra for greasing
1 garlic clove, peeled
5 fresh basil leaves,
  shredded
1 tablespoon fresh
  chopped oregano
50g freshly grated
  Parmesan cheese
200g Taleggio cheese,
  rind removed and cut
  into 12 slices
Salt and white pepper

Baked stuffed tomatoes make a great meat-free meal for summer and are perfect if you're entertaining, as they can be prepared ahead. The filling is a simpler version of the classic saffron-flavoured *risotto alla Milanese* with the addition of Taleggio. It's important to use ripe but firm tomatoes for this dish. Serve with a crispy green salad.

1. Preheat the oven to 180°C/gas mark 4. Put the saffron in a small bowl, add 1 tablespoon of hot water and set aside.

2. Place the rice in a medium saucepan with 1 litre of cold water, add 1 tablespoon of salt and bring to the boil over a high heat. Reduce the heat, cover and simmer gently for 13 minutes or until al dente. Drain thoroughly and set aside.

3. Meanwhile, using a small sharp knife, slice the tops off the tomatoes and reserve. Cut out the pulp (including the seeds) and tip into a medium bowl. Blend the tomato pulp using a hand-held blender until smooth. Brush a deep baking dish, measuring about 38 x 30cm, with oil. Stand the tomato shells upright in the dish.

4. To make the stuffing, heat the oil in a medium saucepan over a medium heat. Add the garlic and fry for 1 minute then discard. Add the blended tomato pulp, the saffron with its soaking liquid and the herbs and season with salt and pepper. Simmer for 10 minutes, stirring occasionally. Remove from the heat and stir in the rice and Parmesan, then taste for seasoning.

5. Half-fill the tomato shells with the stuffing, add a slice of Taleggio, then top up with the remaining stuffing. Replace the tops. Bake for 20–25 minutes. Serve immediately, allowing 2 tomatoes per person.

Most regions in Italy have a coastline, and those that don't have lakes and rivers, so fresh fish is always on the menu. Here I've included a mixture of simple weekday meals for the family and more unusual dishes for entertaining – for instance, the stewed octopus is a real 'wow' for guests. Some of these recipes also make good starters.

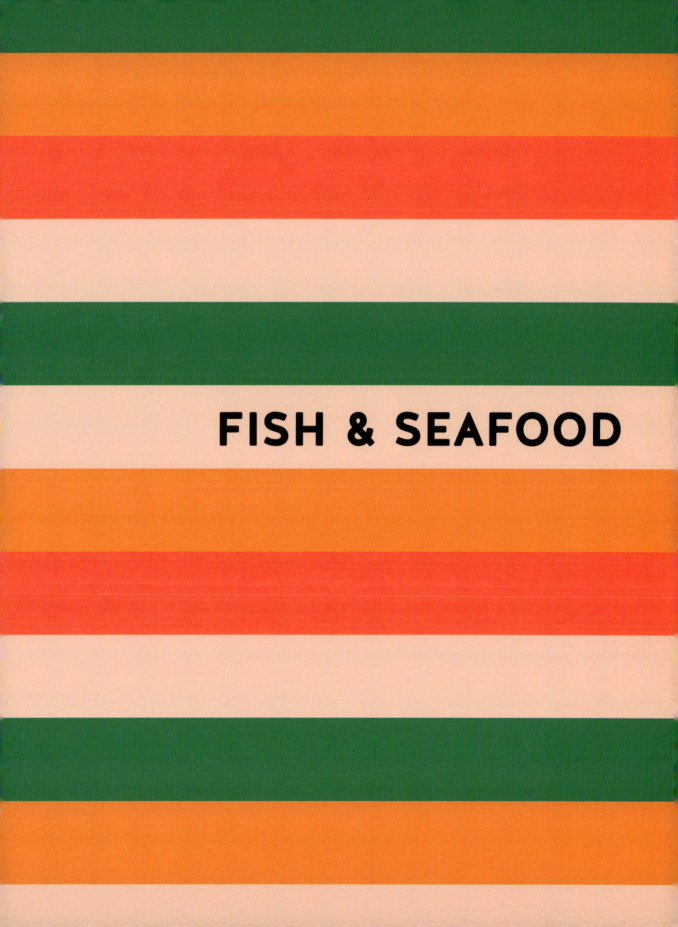

FISH & SEAFOOD

POLENTA-CRUSTED MACKEREL WITH A TOMATO AND BASIL SALAD

Sgombro in crosta di mais con pomodori al basilico

SERVES 4

2 garlic cloves, peeled
Small handful (about 25g) fresh basil leaves
1 unwaxed lemon
75ml extra virgin olive oil
600g fresh mixed cherry or Heirloom tomatoes, halved or quartered
2 large eggs
100g fine polenta
8 fresh mackerel fillets
150ml vegetable oil
Salt and freshly ground black pepper

When I visited Lake Como I met veteran fisherman Ernesto Colombo, who has been fishing the waters for decades. He told me all about agone – the native freshwater fish that arrive on the lake's shores in early summer to spawn. Together we went fly fishing and I cooked our catch right there beside the lake – a real treat. Agone is hard to find in Britain, but mackerel is similar. You can buy mackerel fillets in some supermarkets, but if buying whole mackerel ask your fishmonger to fillet and V-bone them.

1. First make the salad. Use a pestle and mortar to pound the garlic into a paste with some salt and pepper. Add half the basil and pound again. Halve the lemon and squeeze out the juice from one half. Add the juice to the garlic mixture then gradually whisk in the olive oil until well combined. Taste for seasoning. Put the tomatoes in a large bowl, pour over the dressing and stir to coat. Set aside.

2. Crack the eggs into a small bowl, add a pinch of salt and whisk lightly. Spread out the polenta on a large plate. Wipe the mackerel fillets dry with kitchen paper and coat first in the egg and then in the polenta, patting the grains into the egg so they stick.

3. Heat the oil in a large frying pan over a medium to high heat. To test if the oil is ready, add a pinch of polenta to the pan – it will sizzle when the oil is hot enough for frying. Fry the fillets for 1 minute each side or until golden and crisp, remove with a slotted spoon and drain on kitchen paper.

4. Stir the remaining basil into the salad and cut the remaining lemon half into 4 wedges. Place a large spoonful of the tomato salad on a serving plate and arrange 2 mackerel fillets on top. Serve with the lemon wedges.

ROASTED TURBOT WITH POTATOES, TOMATOES AND OLIVES

Rombo al forno con patate, pomodori e olive

SERVES 4-6

800g Maris Piper
   potatoes, peeled and
   cut into 5mm-thick
   slices
6 tablespoons extra
   virgin olive oil
200g fresh red cherry
   tomatoes, halved
1 large red onion,
   peeled and cut into
   5mm-thick slices
150g pitted black olives
   (preferably Taggiasca),
   drained
30g capers, drained
2 tablespoons chopped
   fresh thyme
1 whole turbot, about
   2.2kg
175ml dry white wine
Salt and freshly ground
   black pepper

Turbot is the most popular fish in the region of Friuli-Venezia Giulia, in northeastern Italy. For those of you who haven't tried this highly prized, white-fleshed fish it has a texture similar to halibut – quite meaty and not very bony. This is a simple dish, but make sure you don't overcook the fish or it will become mushy.

1. Preheat the oven to 200°C/gas mark 6. Put the potatoes in a medium saucepan and cover with cold salted water. Bring to the boil and simmer for 3 minutes. Drain and tip back into the same pan. Add 2 tablespoons of the oil, stir to coat and set aside.

2. Put the tomatoes, onion, olives, capers, thyme and the remaining 4 tablespoons of oil in a medium bowl. Season with salt and pepper and stir to combine.

3. Season the turbot with salt and transfer to a large roasting tin, measuring about 40 x 30cm, with the eyes facing up. Arrange the potatoes around the edge and pile the vegetable mixture on top of the potatoes. Pour the wine over the fish.

4. Cook in the oven, uncovered, for 30 minutes (you know the fish is done when the skin comes off easily and the flesh near the bone at the thickest part turns white). Serve immediately.

STUFFED SARDINES

Sarde ripiene

SERVES 8

24 fresh sardines,
   scaled, gutted,
   washed and heads
   removed
24 large fresh basil
   leaves
5 medium eggs
60g plain flour
450g dried
   breadcrumbs
2 litres sunflower oil for
   deep-frying
Salt and freshly ground
   black pepper

For the stuffing
80g pitted green olives
   (preferably Nocellara),
   drained and chopped
1 x 125g ball of
   mozzarella, drained
   and chopped
50g sun-dried tomatoes
   in oil, drained and
   chopped
20g freshly grated
   Parmesan cheese
50g fresh breadcrumbs
½ teaspoon dried
   oregano
½ unwaxed lemon
   (grated zest of half a
   fruit and 1 tablespoon
   juice)

Sardines are good value, plentiful – particularly in summer – and very nutritious, being high in omega 3 and vitamin B. They can be stuffed with practically anything, so feel free to play around with the flavourings in this recipe. Some fishmongers will 'butterfly' the fish for you so it's ready for stuffing. Serve with a salad of your choice and a bottle of chilled beer.

1. First prepare the sardines for stuffing. Open out a fish and place it, skin-side up, on the work surface. Firmly press along the spine until the fish is lying flat. Turn the fish over and carefully pull away the spine, running your finger beneath it to loosen. When you reach the tail-end, cut off the spine using scissors and discard and scrape away any remaining small bones. Rinse the fish under cold running water and pat dry with kitchen paper. Repeat for all the sardines.

2. Put all the ingredients for the stuffing in a medium bowl and stir to combine. Lay a sardine flat on the work surface, skin-side down. Put a large teaspoonful of the stuffing at the head-end of each sardine, place a basil leaf on top, then roll up to enclose. Secure with cocktail sticks. Repeat for all the sardines.

3. Crack the eggs into a small bowl and beat lightly with a fork. Put the flour on a plate and season with salt and pepper. Put the dried breadcrumbs on a separate plate. Carefully coat the sardines, first in the seasoned flour, then in the egg, and finally in the breadcrumbs.

4. Heat a deep-fat fryer to 180°C, or heat the oil in a deep pan or a wok until very hot. To test the temperature, drop a piece of bread into the oil; it will sizzle when the oil is hot enough for frying.

5. Add the sardines and deep-fry for 3 minutes or until golden brown (you will need to fry in batches so they are not touching). Remove with a slotted spoon, drain on kitchen paper and keep warm while you fry the remaining sardines. Arrange the sardines on a large serving platter. Serve immediately.

GRILLED SWORDFISH MARINATED IN LEMON AND FRESH HERBS

Pesce spada alla Pisana

SERVES 4

4 swordfish steaks, about 250g each

8 tablespoons extra virgin olive oil

1 unwaxed lemon (grated zest of ½ lemon, juice of whole fruit)

5 tablespoons chopped fresh flat-leaf parsley

2 tablespoons chopped fresh oregano

Salt and freshly ground black pepper

Swordfish is a good choice for those who aren't usually very keen on fish as it has a firm, meaty texture and the steaks are bone free. Make sure you buy sustainable swordfish from a reputable supplier. If you prefer, you can substitute it with farmed sea bass or halibut. Serve it with Chicory with Spicy Breadcrumbs (see page 148).

1. Lay the swordfish in a shallow, non-metallic dish in a single layer. Combine the remaining ingredients in a small bowl. Pour half the mixture over the fish and set the rest aside.

2. Cover the swordfish and chill for about 1 hour. Remove from the fridge 20 minutes before you are ready to cook.

3. Preheat the grill on a medium setting. Meanwhile, line the grill pan with foil and lay the swordfish in the pan. Grill for about 4–5 minutes each side or until the flesh flakes easily.

4. Place the fish on a large serving platter and drizzle over the reserved marinade. Serve immediately.

Salmone in crosta di erbe, miele e pistacchi

SERVES 4

80g shelled pistachio
nuts

30g fresh white
breadcrumbs

1 tablespoon chopped
fresh rosemary

1 tablespoon chopped
fresh thyme

2 tablespoons chopped
fresh flat-leaf parsley

2 teaspoons runny
honey

1½ tablespoons extra
virgin olive oil, plus
extra for greasing

4 skinned salmon
fillets, about 200g
each

Salt and freshly ground
black pepper

My grandmother, Nonna Flora, used to make this dish every Christmas and for other special occasions; otherwise, we rarely ate salmon and it was a real treat. The pistachios – a Sicilian touch – give great flavour and a nutty texture, and help to keep the fish moist. I have also tried this recipe with cod and it works perfectly. Serve with lemon wedges and Artichokes Braised in Wine (see page 151).

1. Preheat the oven to 180°C/gas mark 4. Chop the pistachios very finely so they are about the same size as the breadcrumbs. Sieve them to remove the dusty skins. Place in a small bowl with the breadcrumbs and herbs and season with salt and pepper. Drizzle over the honey, mix well and set aside.

2. Brush a little oil over the bottom of a baking dish. Place the salmon in the dish and season with salt and pepper. Top one side of the fillets with the pistachio mixture, pressing it down firmly with the back of a spoon.

3. Drizzle with the oil and bake for 25 minutes or until the topping is golden and crisp.

TUNA-STUFFED FENNEL BULBS

Finocchi ripieni di tonno

SERVES 4

4 fennel bulbs (about
  1kg in total), trimmed
3 tablespoons olive oil
1 shallot, peeled and
  finely chopped
60g anchovy fillets
  in oil, drained and
  roughly chopped
100ml dry white wine
1 large courgette (about
  200g), finely chopped
15g capers, drained
40g pitted black olives
  (preferably Leccino),
  drained
200ml hot fish stock
Pinch of saffron
  threads

For the filling
100g stale, rustic-style
  bread, crusts removed
  and torn into bite-
  sized chunks
200ml full-fat milk
400g fresh tuna steaks,
  cut into small bite-
  sized cubes
¼ red onion, peeled and
  finely chopped
1 garlic clove, peeled
  and crushed
2 tablespoons chopped
  fresh flat-leaf parsley
Salt and white pepper

Tuna is very popular in Italy, particularly in central and southern regions. It is often eaten simply grilled, but a Ligurian vegetable seller told me about this recipe that involves stuffing fennel with tuna and I spent a couple of hours with her trying to perfect it – so thank you, Sofia. It's important to use sustainable tuna, ideally approved by the MSC (Marine Stewardship Council). Serve hot with plain rice or at room temperature with a side salad.

1. First make the filling. Put the bread in a medium bowl and pour over the milk. Soak for 20 minutes then squeeze out any excess milk. Return the bread to the bowl and add the tuna, onion, garlic and parsley, along with some salt and pepper. Mix well to combine and set aside.

2. Preheat the oven to 190°C/gas mark 5. Discard the tough outer layers of the fennel. Cut each bulb in half lengthways. Remove the cores, chop finely and set aside. Bring a large pan of salted water to the boil and blanch the fennel halves for 3 minutes. Remove with a slotted spoon and plunge immediately into iced water. When completely cool, drain well and dry thoroughly with kitchen paper. Fill the centre of each fennel half with the tuna mixture and set aside.

3. Heat 1 tablespoon of the oil in a large flameproof casserole over a medium heat. Add the shallot and anchovies and fry for 3 minutes, stirring occasionally, then tip in the chopped fennel cores and fry for 1 minute. Pour in the wine and simmer for about 1 minute or until it has evaporated. Finally, add the courgette, capers, olives, stock and saffron. Bring to a simmer then remove from the heat.

4. Heat the remaining 2 tablespoons of oil in a large frying pan over a medium heat. Add the stuffed fennel, tuna-side down, and fry for 3 minutes or until starting to brown.

5. Transfer the fennel to the casserole, placing it cut-side up and pressing the bulbs lightly into the liquid to submerge them as much as possible. Bake for about 20 minutes (uncovered) or until the fennel is tender and the filling is golden. Serve 2 fennel halves per person with the sauce alongside.

LIGURIAN-STYLE STUFFED SQUID 107

Calamari ripieni alla Ligure

SERVES 6-8

20–22 whole medium
  squid, about 1.6kg in
  total
3 egg whites
120g frozen peas,
  defrosted
1 large red pepper,
  deseeded and cut
  into chunks
2 tablespoons snipped
  fresh chives
3 tablespoons olive oil
1 garlic clove, peeled
100ml dry white wine
400ml passata (sieved
  tomatoes)
250ml hot fish stock
Salt and freshly ground
  black pepper

Squid is so much more versatile than the deep-fried calamari rings that are served in Italian restaurants all over Britain, and this stuffed squid recipe from Liguria is one of my favourites. Make sure you don't overfill the tubes, as during cooking the stuffing expands and the squid shrinks, so you could have an explosion on your hands! You can buy ready-prepared squid, but make sure it comes with the tentacles. Serve with lots of crusty bread to mop up the delicious sauce.

1. To prepare the squid, pull the tentacles from the body. Feel inside the body and remove and discard the 'quill' (a transparent sliver of cartilage). Wash the inside of the body and peel off the outer skin. Cut off the squid tentacles just below the eyes (discard the head and guts). Discard the small, hard 'beak' at the base of the tentacles. Rinse the tentacles in cold water and set aside.

2. Preheat the oven to 190°C/gas mark 5. To make the filling, place 6 squid and the egg whites in a food processor and blitz briefly until roughly chopped. Add the peas, red pepper and chives, season with salt and pepper and blitz again until roughly chopped.

3. Using a cocktail stick, pierce the end of each squid tube (these vent holes will release air and prevent the squid from splitting as it cooks). Spoon a small amount of the filling into each tube until three-quarters full then gently distribute the stuffing with your fingers. Push the tentacles into the end of the tube to seal. Secure with a cocktail stick.

4. Heat the oil in a large flameproof roasting tin, measuring about 40 x 30cm, over a medium heat. Add the garlic and fry for 2 minutes, stirring occasionally. Carefully add the stuffed squid tubes and fry for about 1 minute each side or until they take on a little colour. Pour in the wine and let it simmer for about 1 minute until it evaporates. Add the passata and stock and bring to the boil. Transfer the tin to the oven and cook for 25 minutes or until the squid is tender.

5. Using a slotted spoon, transfer the squid to a bowl. Strain the sauce through a fine sieve into a medium saucepan and place over a high heat. Bring to the boil and simmer for about 5 minutes or until reduced and slightly thickened. Return the squid to the sauce and serve immediately.

Capesante avvolte in pancetta con salsa di avocado

SERVES 4

24 baby spinach leaves
Extra virgin olive oil
   for drizzling
12 fresh medium
   scallops, trimmed
   and corals removed
12 slices of smoked
   pancetta

For the purée
10g salted butter
2 tablespoons olive oil
1 avocado, halved,
   stoned, peeled and
   cut into 2cm cubes
½ garlic clove, crushed
1 sprig of fresh thyme
6 tablespoons hot
   vegetable stock
Salt and freshly ground
   black pepper

Veneto is one of Italy's northernmost provinces, with a long coastline that wraps around the Adriatic Sea. As one might expect given its situation, much of the locals' diet revolves around seafood, including scallops. These little jewels take on the slightly smoky flavour of the pancetta as they cook and, combined with the sweet avocado purée, are a match made in heaven.

1. First make the purée. Heat the butter and olive oil in a small saucepan over a medium heat. Stir in the avocado, garlic and thyme and fry for 4 minutes or until the avocado breaks down. Remove from the heat, discard the thyme sprig and pour over the stock. Using a hand-held blender, blitz to make a smooth sauce then season with some salt and pepper. Return the pan to the hob and keep warm over a very low heat, stirring occasionally.

2. Divide the spinach leaves between 4 serving plates and drizzle over some extra virgin olive oil.

3. Lay a scallop on a slice of pancetta and roll up. Repeat for all the scallops and pancetta. Heat a large frying pan over a high heat. When hot, add the scallops and dry-fry for 1 minute each side. Reduce the heat to medium and fry for a further 1 minute each side. The pancetta should be lightly browned and the scallop cooked but soft in the centre.

4. Place the scallops on the spinach. Spoon over the purée, drizzle with some extra virgin olive oil and grind over a little black pepper. Serve immediately.

SPICY OCTOPUS STEWED IN RED WINE WITH GRILLED PEPPERS

Polpo in umido al vino e peperoni grigliati

SERVES 4

1.5kg frozen raw whole octopus, defrosted overnight in the fridge
2 tablespoons olive oil, plus extra for brushing
3 red onions, peeled and finely sliced
1 teaspoon dried chilli flakes
150ml light red wine
4 teaspoons red wine vinegar
50g anchovy fillets in oil, drained and roughly chopped
1 teaspoon soft brown sugar
2 red peppers, halved lengthways, cored and deseeded
1 orange pepper, halved lengthways, cored and deseeded
1 yellow pepper, halved lengthways, cored and deseeded
2 spring onions, finely sliced
4 tablespoons chopped fresh flat-leaf parsley
Salt

Italians love octopus and it is gradually becoming more popular in Britain. In northern Italy octopus is mostly served cold as an *antipasto* with a dressing, but I like to stew it in wine the southern Italian way. Frozen octopus can be more tender than fresh, as freezing and thawing kick-starts the tenderising process. I've given instructions for prepping, but it can be a messy job so it's best to ask the fishmonger to do it for you.

1. First prepare the octopus. Make one cut at the bottom of the head and another just below the eyes. Discard the central section. Holding the tentacles in one hand, find the hard black 'beak' at their centre. Push the beak through from the underside and discard (if this is tricky, cut around the beak first to loosen). Turn the head inside out and remove and discard the innards.

2. Thoroughly rinse the inside of the head under clean running water and peel away the dark outer skin until you are left with white meat. Rinse the tentacles. Pat dry with kitchen paper. Cut the tentacles from the body and slice between the tentacles to separate them. Cut the body into 4 or 5 pieces.

3. Heat 1 tablespoon of oil in a flameproof casserole over a medium heat. Add the octopus and fry for 1 minute or until the flesh turns pinkish purple (you will need to fry in batches). Transfer to a bowl using a slotted spoon and set aside. Add the remaining tablespoon of oil to the casserole. When hot, add the onions and fry for 10 minutes, stirring occasionally, then add the chilli flakes, wine, vinegar, anchovies and sugar. Stir well then return the octopus and its juices to the casserole. Bring to the boil over a high heat, then reduce the heat to low, cover and simmer for 1 hour or until tender.

4. Meanwhile, preheat the grill for about 5 minutes to medium high. Grill and peel the peppers (see page 18, steps 1 and 2) and cut them into 2cm strips. Keep warm. Using a slotted spoon, transfer the cooked octopus from the casserole to a board and keep warm. Bring the sauce back to the boil then simmer for about 5 minutes or until reduced and slightly thickened. Meanwhile, cut the head and tentacles into bite-sized chunks.

5. To serve, arrange the peppers on a serving platter, put the octopus on top and spoon over the sauce. Scatter over the spring onions and parsley.

Italians probably eat less meat than northern Europeans, but we do love it and cook it in many different ways. Pork and chicken are eaten all over, while beef and veal are favourites in the north and lamb is more popular in central and southern Italy. Here I have selected a great range of meat recipes with unusual and exciting flavour combinations.

POULTRY & MEAT

CHICKEN WITH ANCHOVIES, OLIVES AND CHILLI

Pollo con acciughe, olive e peperoncino

SERVES 4

3 tablespoons plain flour

8 chicken pieces (drumsticks and bone-in thighs), about 1.2kg in total, trimmed

6 tablespoons olive oil

4 anchovy fillets in oil, drained

3 garlic cloves, peeled and crushed

1 sprig of fresh rosemary

2 bay leaves

1 teaspoon dried chilli flakes

100ml balsamic vinegar

100g pitted green olives, drained

200ml passata (sieved tomatoes)

Salt and freshly ground black pepper

Chicken, anchovies and olives are a classic Italian combination dating back hundreds of years. Salted anchovies have been a major export of Liguria since medieval times, and in Piedmont they are so keen on them they have created a hot anchovy dip – rather like fondue – called *bagna cauda*. Here I have used anchovies preserved in olive oil as they are perfect for this recipe and don't need rinsing.

1. Put the flour on a large plate and season with salt and pepper. Dust the chicken with the seasoned flour. Heat the oil in a large flameproof casserole over a medium to high heat. When very hot, add half the chicken and fry for about 5 minutes each side or until golden brown all over. Transfer to a large plate using a slotted spoon and set aside. Repeat for the remaining chicken.

2. Reduce the heat to medium. Add the anchovies, garlic, rosemary and bay leaves and fry for 2 minutes, mashing the anchovies with the back of a spoon, then stir in the chilli flakes.

3. Increase the heat and pour in the vinegar. Bring to the boil and let it bubble rapidly for 1–2 minutes, stirring and scraping the bottom of the pan. Stir in the olives, passata and 100ml of hot water. Season with salt.

4. Return the chicken and its juices to the casserole, pushing the chicken into the sauce to submerge as much as possible. Bring to the boil, then reduce the heat, cover and simmer gently for 30–40 minutes, stirring occasionally, or until the chicken is cooked through and tender.

ROAST CHICKEN STUFFED WITH PASTA

Pollo ripieno di pasta

SERVES 4

1 large whole chicken (about 2kg), giblets removed
200g sliced smoked pancetta
1½ tablespoons olive oil
1 echalion shallot (banana shallot), peeled and finely chopped
150ml dry white wine
200ml passata (sieved tomatoes)
150ml hot chicken stock
100g frozen peas, defrosted
100g dried penne rigate
2 tablespoons chopped fresh flat-leaf parsley
50g freshly grated Parmesan cheese
1 x 125g ball of mozzarella, drained and cut into small cubes
Salt and freshly ground black pepper

When I first saw this dish on a menu in a small town near Turin it seemed such a strange idea I actually laughed out loud. However, it makes perfect sense – the chicken gives the pasta more flavour and the pasta keeps the chicken succulent as it prevents steam from escaping. Serve it with Grilled Vegetables (see page 152).

1. Preheat the oven to 180°C/gas mark 4. Remove any trussing string and place the bird breast-side down on a board with the legs facing you. Using a sharp knife or poultry shears, cut along both sides of the backbone and discard (or save for stock). Turn the chicken over and, using the heel of your hand, press firmly along the breastbone to break it and flatten the bird. Set aside.

2. Finely dice half the pancetta and set the rest aside. Heat the oil in a medium saucepan over a medium heat. Add the shallot and fry for 5 minutes, then add the diced pancetta and fry for 3 minutes, stirring frequently. Increase the heat, pour in the wine, bring to the boil and let it bubble rapidly for 1–2 minutes. Add the passata and stock and bring to the boil, then reduce the heat and simmer for 5 minutes, stirring occasionally. Tip in the peas and simmer for 5 minutes. Remove from the heat and set aside.

3. Bring a medium saucepan of salted water to the boil and cook the penne for half the time stated on the packet. Drain the pasta then tip it into the sauce. Stir in the parsley and Parmesan. Let cool then stir in the mozzarella.

4. Season inside and out with salt and pepper. Spoon about three-quarters of the pasta mixture into the main cavity. Seal with skewers or cocktail sticks. Tie the legs together with string. Turn the chicken over and spoon the remaining pasta and sauce into the neck end. Pull the neck skin over the neck cavity and secure with skewers or cocktail sticks. Tie the wings to the breast with string.

5. Put the chicken breast-side up in a large deep roasting tin, measuring about 30 x 25cm, and roast for about 1 hour. Remove from the oven, lay the pancetta slices over the chicken and cook for a further 10–15 minutes or until the juices run clear when the flesh is pierced with a sharp knife in the thickest part of the breast. Transfer the chicken to a large, warmed serving platter and cover with foil. Leave to rest for 10 minutes then carve into thick slices.

CHICKEN WITH LEMON AND FRESH ROSEMARY

Pollo al limone e rosmarino

SERVES 4

3 tablespoons plain
flour
8 chicken pieces
(drumsticks and bone-
in thighs), about 1.2kg
in total, trimmed
6 tablespoons olive oil
1 large onion, peeled
and chopped
3 celery sticks,
chopped
3 carrots, peeled and
chopped
2 garlic cloves, peeled
and crushed
6 sprigs of fresh
rosemary
4 bay leaves
100ml dry white wine
500ml hot chicken
stock
1 unwaxed lemon
Salt and white pepper

Italians love the combination of chicken, lemon, garlic and rosemary. A native Mediterranean herb, rosemary not only gives dishes a wonderful flavour and aroma but also has incredible health benefits. It's a good source of iron, calcium and Vitamin B6 and is believed to have anti-inflammatory and tumour-fighting properties. In fact, a current research project into a southern Italian community where 15 per cent of the population are centenarians suggests the longevity of the inhabitants may be due to the large amounts of rosemary they use in their cooking.

1. Put the flour on a large plate and season with salt and pepper. Dust the chicken with the seasoned flour. Heat the oil in a large flameproof casserole over a medium to high heat. When very hot, add half the chicken, skin-side down, and fry for about 5 minutes each side or until golden brown all over. Transfer to a large plate using a slotted spoon and set aside. Repeat for the remaining chicken.

2. Reduce the heat to medium. Add the onion, celery, carrots, garlic, rosemary and bay leaves. Fry for 15 minutes, stirring occasionally.

3. Increase the heat and pour in the wine. Bring to the boil and let it bubble rapidly for 1–2 minutes, stirring and scraping the bottom of the pan to release any sticky bits left from the chicken. Add the stock and bring to the boil.

4. Return the chicken and its juices to the casserole. Squeeze the juice from the lemon over the chicken and put the spent shells in the casserole. Season with salt and pepper. Bring to the boil, then reduce the heat, cover and simmer gently for 30–40 minutes or until the chicken is cooked through and tender, stirring occasionally. Serve immediately.

Petti d'anatra con salsa di ciliegie e vino

SERVES 4

400g cherries, halved and stoned
Juice of 2-3 large oranges, about 160ml
100g caster sugar
500ml full-bodied red wine (preferably Barolo)
4 duck breasts
Salt and white pepper

Cherries are very popular in Italy – particularly in Emilia-Romagna and Veneto, where there is a famous local cherry festival (*Sagra delle Ciliegie*) in the old town of Marostica from May to June each year. Out of season you can use frozen cherries – defrost them thoroughly and cook them for a further 10 minutes. Serve with creamy mashed potato and Green Beans with Balsamic and Garlic (see page 147).

1. Preheat the oven to 180°C/gas mark 4. Put the cherries in a small baking dish with the orange juice and half the sugar and bake for 25 minutes or until the cherries have softened. Remove from the oven and set aside. Increase the oven temperature to 200°C/gas mark 6.

2. Pour the wine into a medium saucepan and add the remaining sugar. Heat over a low heat for several minutes until the sugar has dissolved, stirring occasionally. Increase the heat and bring to the boil. Boil for about 1 minute. Reduce the heat and simmer for 35-40 minutes or until syrupy and reduced by about two-thirds. Set aside.

3. Pat the duck dry with kitchen paper. Using a sharp knife, score the skin by making 4 or 5 diagonal cuts to the point where you can see the flesh. Season both sides with salt and pepper.

4. Place a large non-stick frying pan over a high heat and when hot place the duck breasts in the pan, skin-side down, and cook for 5-6 minutes without disturbing them. Drain off all the fat. Turn the duck and brown the other side for 30 seconds. Transfer to a small roasting tin, skin-side up, and cook in the oven for 8-10 minutes.

5. Meanwhile, make the sauce. Put the reduced wine and the cherries with their sugary juices in a medium frying pan. Bring to the boil over a high heat, then reduce the heat and simmer for 5-10 minutes or until reduced by about one-third.

6. To serve, cut the duck into slices, about 5mm thick, and arrange on a large serving platter. Spoon over the sauce and serve immediately.

MARSALA QUAIL WITH PARSLEY MASH
Quaglie al marsala con purè al prezzemolo

SERVES 4

4 quail
1kg large red potatoes
 (preferably Mozart)
2 tablespoons chopped
 fresh flat-leaf parsley
Salt and freshly ground
 black pepper

For the marinade
40g sultanas
1 teaspoon sweet
 smoked paprika
1 tablespoon chopped
 fresh rosemary
3 tablespoons extra
 virgin olive oil
175ml Marsala wine
1 tablespoon red
 wine vinegar

Italians love game, with the shooting season starting the first Sunday of September and finishing at the end of November. Whole quail make an impressive dinner party dish, but they can be fiddly to eat, which is why I've come up with this boned, stuffed recipe. As the meat is very lean it can be dry, but marinating makes it more succulent as well as adding flavour. For ease, ask your butcher to spatchcock the birds for you. Serve with baby carrots and mangetouts.

1. To spatchcock the quail, remove any trussing string and place the bird breast-side down on a board with the legs facing you. Using a sharp knife or poultry shears, cut along both sides of the backbone and discard. Turn the quail over and, using the heel of your hand, press along the breastbone to break it and flatten the bird. Lay the quail in a large, shallow, non-metallic dish.

2. Put all the ingredients for the marinade in a small bowl and grind over some pepper. Stir to combine. Pour the marinade evenly over the quail. Cover and chill for at least 8 hours, preferably overnight.

3. Preheat the oven to 180°C/gas mark 4. Score a cross in each potato. Place the potatoes in a roasting tin and bake for about 1 hour or until soft when pierced with a knife. Set aside.

4. Preheat the grill for about 5 minutes on its highest setting. Lift the quail out of the marinade (reserve the marinade) and transfer the birds breast-side down to a large grill pan or roasting tin, measuring about 40 x 30cm.

5. Grill the quail for 15 minutes, then turn over and cook for a further 10 minutes or until golden. Meanwhile, pour the reserved marinade into a small saucepan and bring to the boil on the hob, then reduce the heat and simmer gently, stirring occasionally. Keep warm.

6. Remove the quail from the tin, cover with foil and leave to rest for 10 minutes. Meanwhile, cut the potatoes in half and scoop out the flesh into a medium bowl. Discard the skins. Add the parsley, season with salt and pepper, and gently mash using a potato masher until smooth. Serve the quail with the mash alongside. Drizzle over the warmed marinade and serve immediately.

SALUMI & SALUMERIE

Whenever I visit a new town in Italy the first thing I do is head straight to the local *salumeria* (delicatessen). I'm like a child in a sweet shop – the vast array of cured meats is incredible, and because each region in Italy has its own specialities there is always something new and exciting to discover. The process of air-drying, salting and smoking meats started out of necessity well over two thousand years ago to prevent food spoilage and disease, but today cured meats are valued for their wonderful flavours and textures. Known collectively as *salumi* in Italy, cured meats fall into two categories: those made from a single cut of an animal – usually a shoulder or hind leg, as with prosciutto – and those that contain ground meat stuffed into a casing with other flavourings, as with salamis and *salsicce* (sausages). Pork is the most common meat for curing, but beef, goat, wild boar and venison – even donkey and horse – are also cured in some regions. In Italy, cured meats are usually served as part of an *affettato* (platter of sliced meats) – although some kinds are used in cooking.

Cured meats are popular throughout Italy, with those in the north generally milder in flavour than the southern versions, which often contain chillies and can be extremely spicy. Here is a selection of my favourites.

Bresaola A speciality of Lombardy, bresaola is raw fillet of beef that has been salted then air dried for several months. It is sliced paper-thin and has a sweet flavour.

Coppa Cured pork shoulder from northern Italy with a delicate flavour and texture. There is a spicy version, known as capocollo, from Campania.

Guanciale A speciality of central Italy (especially Umbria and Lazio), this is pork cheek that has been salted, rolled in pepper and dried. It has a strong flavour and is good for cooking (see page 59), but is also eaten raw.

Mocetta In the Val d'Aosta and neighbouring Alpine regions boned thigh of goat is marinated in wine with juniper berries and other flavourings and then salted and cured. Other meats are sometimes used.

Mortadella Large pink sausage made from heat-cured pork. It originated in Bologna but is now made elsewhere in northern Italy. It is traditionally flavoured with myrtle.

Pancetta Salt-cured pork belly, similar to bacon. There are two types: Pancetta arrotolata is rolled and eaten raw, pancetta tesa is flat and used in cooking. It can also be smoked.

Prosciutto cotto Cooked ham produced in northern Italy (generally, cooked ham is not eaten in the south).

Prosciutto crudo Sweet-flavoured cured ham produced in northern and central Italy, with prosciutto from Parma and San Daniele being the most famous kinds. The pig's thigh is salted and aged for about 14 months, sometimes longer.

Speck A speciality of the mountainous region of Trentino-Alto Adige, speck is a type of Tyrolean smoked prosciutto that is eaten as an *antipasto* or used in cooking (see page 62).

AROMATIC MEAT STEW WITH RED WINE, CLOVES AND JUNIPER BERRIES

Bollito di carne

SERVES 8

140ml olive oil
4 duck legs (about 800g in total), skinned, trimmed and cut into drumsticks and thighs
800g pork spare ribs, cut into 2-rib sections
1kg bone-in chicken thighs, skinned and trimmed
1 large red onion, peeled and roughly chopped
1 celery stick, roughly chopped
1 carrot, peeled and roughly chopped
2 cloves
8 juniper berries
300ml full-bodied red wine
3 tablespoons chopped fresh flat-leaf parsley
1 litre hot vegetable stock
2 tablespoons tomato purée
Salt and freshly ground black pepper

Bollito di carne is a classic northern Italian dish, typically from Piedmont. Hearty, rich and satisfying, it always includes several different types of meat – the kinds used vary depending on availability and the preference of the cook. For this recipe I decided to use duck, pork and chicken, as recommended to me by a butcher in one of the markets I visited when filming in Piedmont. Serve with plenty of toasted sliced ciabatta rubbed with fresh garlic on both sides.

1. Heat half the oil in a large flameproof casserole over a medium to high heat. When very hot, fry the duck, pork and chicken in batches until well browned on all sides. Remove the meat with a slotted spoon and transfer to a large bowl. Set aside.

2. Pour in the remaining oil and reduce the heat to medium. Add the onion, celery, carrot, cloves and juniper berries and fry for about 5–10 minutes, stirring occasionally.

3. Increase the heat, pour in the wine and add the parsley. Bring to the boil and let it bubble for 1–2 minutes. Add the stock and tomato purée and bring to the boil.

4. Return the meat to the pan with any juices. Season with salt and pepper. Bring to the boil then reduce the heat, cover and simmer gently for 1–1½ hours or until the meat is tender, stirring occasionally.

COUNTRY-STYLE PORK RIBS

Costolette di maiale

SERVES 4

3 tablespoons plain flour

1.3kg pork spare ribs, cut into 2-rib sections

6 tablespoons olive oil

1 onion, peeled and finely chopped

2 garlic cloves, peeled and crushed

2 tablespoons chopped fresh rosemary

15 fresh sage leaves, shredded

3 bay leaves

200ml dry white wine

300ml hot vegetable stock

1 x 400g tin of chopped tomatoes

¼ teaspoon freshly grated nutmeg

Salt and freshly ground black pepper

The first time I ate this dish was in a farmhouse in the Emilia-Romagna region, when I was filming *Gino's Italian Escape*, and it has stayed with me ever since. The fact that the pork is slow-cooked, on the bone, means that the meat is incredibly flavourful and tender. Serve with crusty bread to mop up the delicious sauce.

1. Put the flour on a large plate and season with salt and pepper. Dust the ribs with the seasoned flour. Heat half the oil in a large saucepan over a medium to high heat. When very hot, fry the ribs in batches for about 3 minutes each side or until browned all over. Remove with a slotted spoon and transfer to a large bowl or plate. Set aside.

2. Pour in the remaining oil and reduce the heat to medium. Add the onion, garlic and herbs and fry for 6 minutes, stirring occasionally.

3. Increase the heat and pour in the wine. Bring to the boil and let it bubble for 1–2 minutes. Add the stock and tomatoes and bring to the boil, stirring.

4. Return the ribs to the pan with any juices. Reduce the heat, cover and simmer for 1 hour or until the meat is tender and the sauce slightly thickened. Season with salt and pepper and stir in the nutmeg. Serve immediately.

GRILLED LAMB SKEWERS WITH A GREEN BEAN AND GOAT'S CHEESE SALAD

Arrosticini con insalata di fagiolini e caprino

SERVES 4

600g lamb loin fillet, cut into 3cm cubes

100ml extra virgin olive oil, plus extra for drizzling

4 teaspoons runny honey

1 tablespoon fennel seeds

Small handful (about 25g) of chopped fresh mint

300g fine green beans, trimmed

125g soft goat's cheese

25g pine nuts

1 yellow pepper, deseeded and cut into 3cm pieces

1 red pepper, deseeded and cut into 3cm pieces

½ lemon

Salt and freshly ground black pepper

Situated in the heart of the Apennines, Abruzzo is a largely mountainous region straddled between central and southern Italy. It has a long, historic tradition of sheep farming, as I learned from the farmer Mauro, who took me out shepherding with him. As you would expect, lamb is the favourite meat of the area, with *arrosticini* (grilled skewered lamb) being the local speciality. Here is my take on the dish, using a barbecue to create the effect of an Italian-style outdoor grill, served with a salad accompaniment. If you haven't got a barbecue, cook the meat under a hot grill for 5 minutes.

1. Put the lamb in a medium bowl. Add the oil, honey, fennel seeds, mint and some salt and pepper and stir to combine. Set aside.

2. To make the salad, bring a small saucepan of salted water to the boil and cook the beans for 3 minutes or until just tender. Drain and rinse under cold running water (so they retain their crunch), then drain again thoroughly. Put the green beans in a bowl while they are still warm, crumble over the goat's cheese and season with salt and pepper. Sprinkle over the pine nuts and drizzle over a little olive oil.

3. Light the barbecue. Thread 4 metal skewers, 25cm long, with the lamb and the peppers. Brush over any excess marinade.

4. When the barbecue is ready (the coals will be covered in a fine greyish white ash) place the skewers on the barbecue and grill for about 4–5 minutes each side or until the meat is cooked through and the peppers are starting to char. Serve the skewers with a squeeze of lemon juice and the salad alongside.

LAMB CUTLETS BAKED WITH POTATOES, ARTICHOKES AND GARLIC

Costine di agnello con carciofi, patate e aglio

SERVES 4

4 tablespoons olive oil
12 lamb cutlets,
    trimmed
3 large Desirée
    potatoes, peeled and
    cut into chunky chips
3 garlic cloves, peeled
    and left whole
100ml dry white wine
400ml hot vegetable
    stock
350g chargrilled
    artichoke hearts in
    oil, drained and
    halved lengthways
Salt and freshly ground
    black pepper

Most of Italy's lamb is raised in the southern and central regions of Lazio and Abruzzo, where the land is hilly and rocky and better suited to grazing sheep than cattle. Abruzzo cuisine features a lot of lamb, often combining it with artichokes in spring, when lamb is at its most tender. Serve with a beautiful bottle of Italian red wine.

1. Preheat the oven to 180°C/gas mark 4. Heat 2 tablespoons of the oil in a large frying pan over a medium to high heat. Add the lamb and fry for 2 minutes each side or until golden brown (you will probably have to fry in batches). Transfer to a large deep roasting tin or baking dish measuring about 30 x 40cm. Set the frying pan aside.

2. Bring a medium saucepan of salted water to the boil. Add the potatoes, bring to the boil and simmer for 2 minutes. Drain thoroughly. Arrange the potatoes on top of the lamb in a single layer.

3. Bruise the garlic by placing each clove under the flat side of a knife and pressing down with your palm to crush it slightly. Return the frying pan to a medium heat. Add the garlic and fry for 2 minutes. Increase the heat and pour in the wine. Bring to the boil and let it bubble for 1–2 minutes. Add the stock and bring to the boil, then pour the liquid over the potatoes. Season with salt and pepper. Drizzle over the remaining 2 tablespoons of oil. Bake for 20 minutes.

4. Remove the tin from the oven and lay the artichokes over the potatoes in a single layer. Return to the oven and bake for a further 15 minutes. Serve immediately.

Agnello al forno con gratin alle erbe

SERVES 4

1 shoulder of lamb (about 2kg) on the bone
2 tablespoons olive oil
1 tablespoon tomato purée
1 x 750ml bottle of full-bodied red wine
1 litre hot chicken stock
4 cloves
4 bay leaves
1 whole head of garlic
1kg fluffy potatoes (preferably King Edward), peeled and cut into 3cm chunks
600g carrots, peeled and cut into 2cm-thick rounds
Salt and freshly ground black pepper

For the crust
100g fresh white breadcrumbs
2 tablespoons chopped fresh flat-leaf parsley
1 tablespoon chopped fresh mint
1 teaspoon dried marjoram
3 tablespoons freshly grated Grana Padano cheese
4 tablespoons extra virgin olive oil

Traditionally, roast lamb is eaten throughout Italy on Easter Sunday – even in regions where lamb isn't eaten much the rest of the year. I particularly like roasting lamb shoulder that has been coated in a tasty herb crust and cooked low and slow, as in this recipe – it's so sweet and succulent.

1. Put all the ingredients for the crust in a medium bowl. Stir thoroughly to combine. Set aside.

2. Season the lamb with salt and pepper. Heat the olive oil in a large, high-sided frying pan over a high heat. When very hot, fry the lamb for 4–5 minutes each side until golden brown. Drain off any fat and discard. Transfer the lamb to a large flameproof roasting tin measuring about 40 x 30cm. Preheat the oven to 160°C/gas mark 3.

3. Return the frying pan to the hob over a high heat and add the tomato purée, wine, stock, cloves and bay leaves. Bring to the boil then simmer until reduced by half. Pour the liquid over the lamb. Cover the tin with foil and put in the oven for 1½ hours, basting occasionally.

4. Remove the tin from the oven and pour three quarters of the liquid into a small saucepan. Bring to the boil over a high heat and simmer until reduced by half (this will be the gravy). Set aside.

5. Meanwhile, slice off the top 10mm of the garlic to expose the cloves and put the whole head in the roasting tin with the lamb. Arrange the potatoes and carrots around the lamb. Season with salt and pepper. Return the tin to the oven (uncovered) and roast for 1 hour.

6. Preheat the grill for about 5 minutes on its highest setting. Cover the top of the lamb with the crust mixture, pressing down firmly. Transfer the lamb to a grill pan and grill for about 2 minutes or until the crust is golden brown.

7. Squeeze the flesh from the roasted garlic cloves into the gravy and stir. Pour the gravy into a jug and serve alongside the lamb and roasted vegetables.

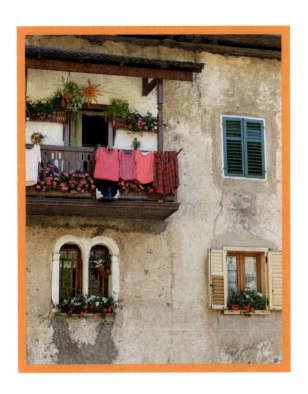

Schiaccicia
piccante
€ 14.72 al/Kg

MORTADELLA
FEGATO
€ 11.60 al/Kg

PANCETTA
ARROTOLATA
€ 11.80 al/Kg

LARDO
€ 11.50 al/Kg

CRESPONE
€ 15.93 al/Kg

SALAME
MILANO
€ 15.93 al/Kg

SOPRESSATA
CALABRESE
€ 12.90 al/Kg

PANCETTA
TESA PEPE
o AFFUMICATA
€ 11.99 al/Kg

TACCHINO
ARROSTO
€ 15.90 al/Kg

VEAL WITH A TUNA, ANCHOVY AND CAPER MAYONNAISE

Vitello tonnato

SERVES 6

1 veal fillet, about 600g
4 tablespoons extra
  virgin olive oil, plus
  extra for drizzling
300g tuna chunks in
  oil (tinned or in a jar),
  drained
4 anchovy fillets in oil,
  drained
20 capers, drained
200g mayonnaise
4 tablespoons chopped
  fresh flat-leaf parsley
Salt and white pepper

A classic dish from Piedmont, this consists of cold, sliced veal covered with a creamy, piquant tuna sauce. It's usually served in summer as a main course, but many serve it as part of the *antipasti* table. I know it sounds a little odd, but please trust me on this one – I guarantee it's *fantastico*! My friend Matt Kay (also known as Jerry Maguire) really loves this dish, so Matt – this one is for you. Serve with slices of toasted ciabatta rubbed on both sides with garlic.

1. Preheat the oven to 200°C/gas mark 6. Place the veal in a roasting tin, drizzle over a little oil and roast for 20 minutes. Remove the meat from the tin and set aside to cool completely.

2. Using a sharp knife, slice the veal very thinly and arrange the slices on a serving platter. Season with salt and pepper.

3. Put the tuna, anchovies and half the capers in a food processor and blitz until smooth. Gradually blend in the 4 tablespoons of oil then add the mayonnaise. The consistency should be like thick double cream; if necessary, add a little cold water to make the sauce slightly runnier. Transfer to a bowl, stir in the parsley and season with salt and pepper.

4. Pour the tuna mayonnaise over the veal and sprinkle over the remaining capers. Serve at room temperature.

CLASSIC OSSO BUCO WITH GREMOLATA

Osso buco con gremolata

SERVES 6

3 tablespoons plain
   white flour
6 veal shanks (about
   300–400g each),
   trimmed
6 tablespoons olive oil
1 large onion, peeled
   and finely chopped
4 celery sticks, finely
   chopped
1 large carrot, peeled
   and finely chopped
2 garlic cloves, peeled
   and crushed
3 bay leaves
2 strips of lemon zest,
   about 10cm long
2 sprigs of fresh
   rosemary
600ml dry white wine
150ml hot vegetable
   stock
1 tablespoon tomato
   purée
Salt and freshly ground
   black pepper

For the gremolata
6 tablespoons chopped
   fresh flat-leaf parsley
1 tablespoon chopped
   fresh rosemary
Grated zest of 1
   unwaxed lemon

A Milanese speciality, *osso buco* (slow-cooked veal shank) is traditionally served with *risotto alla milanese* (saffron risotto) and garnished with *gremolata*. *Osso buco* means 'bone with a hole', referring to the hole at the centre of the shank. Traditionally, the bone marrow is lifted out with a toothpick so it can be savoured. Veal shanks can be difficult to find in supermarkets so you may have to order them from a butcher. Baked Polenta (see page 159) makes an excellent accompaniment.

1. Preheat the oven to 180°C/gas mark 4. Put the flour on a large plate and season with salt and pepper. Dust the veal with the seasoned flour.

2. Heat half the oil in a large flameproof casserole over a medium to high heat. When very hot, add half the veal shanks and fry for about 3–4 minutes each side or until golden brown all over. Transfer to a large plate using a slotted spoon and set aside. Repeat for the remaining veal.

3. Reduce the heat to medium. Pour in the remaining oil. When hot, add the onion, celery, carrot, garlic, bay leaves, lemon zest and rosemary. Fry for 5 minutes, stirring occasionally.

4. Increase the heat and pour in the wine. Bring to the boil and let it bubble for 5 minutes. Add the stock and tomato purée and bring to the boil. Return the veal to the casserole, submerging it in the liquid, and bring back to the boil, stirring. Cover and transfer the casserole to the oven. After 30 minutes, remove the lid and cook for 1 further hour uncovered. The veal should be very tender and the sauce thickened.

5. Meanwhile, to make the gremolata, put the parsley, rosemary and lemon zest in a small bowl and season with pepper. Stir to combine.

6. To serve, place a veal shank on a serving plate, spoon the sauce around and sprinkle over the gremolata.

SLICED STEAK WITH TRUFFLE BUTTER

Tagliata con burro al tartufo

SERVES 6

200g good-quality salted butter (room temperature)
50g black summer truffles (25g finely grated, 25g very thinly sliced)
140g rocket leaves
2 tablespoons extra virgin olive oil, plus extra for brushing
6 sirloin steaks, about 150g each
Sea salt flakes

Italians love a good steak and serve it in a number of ways. Sometimes it's served in one large piece – such as the famous Florentine *bistecca* – but frequently it's simply grilled then carved, in which case it is known as *tagliata*. Topped with truffle butter made from black summer truffles (see the recipe introduction on page 56), this steak is ideal for a special occasion. Remember to remove the meat from the fridge 20 minutes before cooking. Try this with my Taggiasca Olive Bread (see page 185).

1. To make the truffle butter, put the butter in a small bowl with the grated truffles and beat together with a small wooden spoon. Transfer to a sheet of cling film and roll up to make a cylinder. Twist the ends to seal and chill until firm (at least 1 hour). Discard the cling film and slice the butter into 1cm-thick rounds. Return to the fridge.

2. In a medium bowl toss the rocket with the oil and arrange on a large flat serving platter. Preheat a ridged cast-iron chargrill pan over a high heat for 5–10 minutes or until piping hot. Meanwhile, wipe the steaks dry with kitchen paper, brush both sides with a little oil and season with pepper.

3. Place 2 steaks in the pan and grill for 2 minutes, pressing down with a fish slice but not moving them around. Turn over and place a slice of the truffle butter on top of each steak then sprinkle over a pinch of salt. Grill for a further 2 minutes for rare. Lift the steaks out of the pan and leave to rest. Repeat for the remaining steaks, allowing the last batch to rest for 2 minutes.

4. To serve, cut the steak diagonally into slices about 5mm thick and arrange on the rocket. Scatter over the sliced truffles.

The vegetables in Italy are amazing – so fresh and full of flavour – and I love the fact that when you shop in the local market you'll find only seasonal produce (you'll never see asparagus in winter for instance). Italians usually serve side dishes on individual plates, separate from the main dinner plate, so each dish can retain its own flavour.

VEGETABLES & SIDES

GREEN BEANS WITH BALSAMIC AND GARLIC

Fagiolini alla Modenese

SERVES 6

4 tablespoons balsamic vinegar

3 garlic cloves, crushed

4 tablespoons extra virgin olive oil

1kg fine green beans, trimmed

Salt and freshly ground black pepper

Italians love green beans and grow many different kinds, some of which are purplish and mottled or yellow rather than bright green. One variety – which is known as asparagus bean (Fagiolino di Sant'Anna) and originates in Tuscany – has incredibly long pods, measuring 30–50cm – they look amazing! For this recipe I have used the more familiar fine green beans, which you can buy in any British supermarket. It's my favourite green bean recipe of all time and is fantastic with fish.

1. Put the vinegar and garlic in a small bowl and gradually whisk in the oil. Season with salt and pepper and set aside.

2. Bring a large saucepan of salted water to the boil. Drop the beans into the water, bring back to the boil and simmer for 4 minutes or until just tender. Drain and rinse under cold running water (so they retain their crunch), then drain again thoroughly.

3. Tip the beans back into the pan. Pour over the dressing and toss well. Transfer the beans to a large bowl and serve immediately.

CHICORY WITH SPICY BREADCRUMBS

Cicoria con pan grattato piccante

SERVES 6

6 tablespoons olive oil
2 garlic cloves, cut in half lengthways (skin left on)
½ teaspoon dried chilli flakes
3 tablespoons fresh white breadcrumbs
300g white chicory, cut into 2cm pieces
Salt

It was a Belgian who first brought chicory to the northern Italian region of Veneto in the 19th century, and since then Italians have become true connoisseurs of this wonderful ingredient. In season in autumn and winter, chicory has an intriguing, bitter flavour and makes a delicious and unusual side dish, particularly with fish.

1. Heat 3 tablespoons of the oil in a medium frying pan over a medium heat. Add the garlic and fry for 2 minutes or until golden brown then discard. Add the chilli flakes, breadcrumbs and some salt and fry for 3 minutes, stirring constantly, until the crumbs are golden. Remove from the heat and tip the mixture immediately into a bowl. Set aside.

2. Bring a medium saucepan of salted water to the boil. Add the chicory, bring back to the boil and simmer for about 4 minutes or until tender. Drain thoroughly in a sieve or colander, pressing hard on the chicory with the back of a spoon to extract as much water as possible.

3. Heat the remaining 3 tablespoons of oil in a medium frying pan over a high heat. Tip in the chicory and fry for 2 minutes, stirring occasionally. Add the breadcrumb mixture and stir to combine. Serve immediately.

Carciofi brasati al vino bianco

SERVES 6

6 garlic cloves, peeled and roughly chopped

2 tablespoons roughly chopped fresh flat-leaf parsley

2 tablespoons roughly chopped fresh mint

1 teaspoon coarse sea salt

12 medium globe artichokes

1 lemon, quartered

5 tablespoons extra virgin olive oil

150ml dry white wine

Salt and freshly ground black pepper

Artichokes are incredibly popular in the regions of Lazio, Tuscany, Umbria and Liguria. Very tender young artichokes are often eaten raw in salads, or preserved in oil, while larger artichokes are most often sautéed, stuffed, fried or breaded. This dish can be served as part of the *antipasti* table as well as a side dish.

1. Use a pestle and mortar to mash the garlic, parsley, mint and sea salt to a coarse paste. Set aside.

2. Clean the artichokes and remove the dark, tough outer leaves. Using a sharp knife cut off the top third of the artichoke and trim the stalk to 2–3cm long. Pull back the leaves to expose the hairy choke at the centre. Use a teaspoon to scoop it out and discard. Rub all cut surfaces of the artichoke with the lemon to prevent discoloration. Divide the pounded herb mixture between the artichokes, pressing it into the central cavity.

3. Heat the oil in a large wide saucepan or sauté pan over a medium heat. Add the artichokes, cut-side down, and fry for 2 minutes or until lightly browned. Increase the heat slightly, pour in the wine and simmer for 1–2 minutes or until it has evaporated.

4. Add 150ml of warm water and bring to the boil. Reduce the heat to low, cover and simmer for about 40 minutes or until tender, basting with the pan juices occasionally. Add a little extra hot water if the artichokes look like they are drying out.

5. Put the artichokes in a serving bowl and season with salt and pepper. Drizzle over the pan juices. Serve warm.

GRILLED VEGETABLES WITH A HONEY, CHILLI AND HERB DRESSING

Verdure grigliate condite con miele, erbe e peperoncino

SERVES 6

Olive oil for brushing
1 large fennel bulb,
  cored and cut into
  8 wedges
1 large leek, sliced into
  1.5cm-thick rounds
2 red peppers,
  deseeded and cut into
  6 wedges
2 yellow peppers,
  deseeded and cut into
  6 wedges
1 aubergine, sliced into
  1.5cm-thick rounds
2 large plum tomatoes,
  cut into 4 wedges
2 courgettes, cut into
  1cm-slices and halved
Salt

For the dressing
75ml red wine vinegar
2 teaspoons runny
  honey
150ml extra virgin
  olive oil
2 garlic cloves, peeled
  and finely sliced
1 fresh, medium-hot red
  chilli, deseeded and
  finely chopped
12 fresh mint leaves,
  finely shredded
1 tablespoon fresh
  oregano leaves
½ teaspoon salt

Barbecued vegetables, with their lovely smoky flavour, go beautifully with plain fish and meat dishes. If you don't have a garden barbecue, disposable barbecues are available in most supermarkets and are usually reasonably priced. Alternatively, use a ridged, cast-iron chargrill pan for this recipe. Don't throw away any leftovers as these vegetables are also delicious eaten cold the next day.

1. Light the barbecue and preheat the oven to 190°C/gas mark 5. Meanwhile, make the dressing. Put the vinegar and honey in a small bowl and gradually whisk in the oil. Stir in the garlic, chilli, herbs and salt. Set aside.

2. Brush some oil over the fennel and leek and season with salt and pepper. When the barbecue is ready (the coals will be covered in a fine greyish white ash) grill the fennel and leek for about 5 minutes each side or until charred. Transfer to a baking sheet and put in the oven for 10 minutes.

3. Brush the remaining vegetables with oil, season with salt and pepper and grill on the barbecue for about 3 minutes each side or until charred.

4. Put all the vegetables on a large serving platter and pour over the dressing. Lightly toss and leave for a few minutes so the vegetables can soak up the flavour. Serve hot, warm or at room temperature.

ROASTED NEW POTATOES WITH LECCINO OLIVES

Patate arrosto con olive Leccino

SERVES 6

1kg baby new potatoes, scrubbed

1 red pepper, deseeded and sliced into 1cm-thick strips

1 yellow pepper, deseeded and sliced into 1cm-thick strips

8 garlic cloves, unpeeled and left whole

2 large sprigs of fresh rosemary

200ml extra virgin olive oil

1 tablespoon coarse sea salt

½ teaspoon freshly ground black pepper

100g pitted black Leccino olives, drained

Italy's landscape is dotted with olive trees (more than 50 different varieties are grown throughout the country) so it is no surprise that olives feature in so many Italian dishes. Leccino olives – which originated in Tuscany but are now widespread – are small and black, with a nutty flavour that complements these potatoes beautifully. They're one of the main types used to make olive oil, but are also great for cooking and with an *aperitivo*. This recipe is ideal for lazy days when a good side dish is needed with minimum effort, and it's easy to make a double batch for big get-togethers.

1. Preheat the oven to 200°C/gas mark 6. Place the potatoes, peppers, garlic and rosemary in a large baking dish.

2. Pour over the oil, sprinkle with the salt and pepper and toss together until thoroughly combined. Roast for 15 minutes. Turn the vegetables then add the olives and roast for a further 20 minutes. Serve immediately.

OVEN-ROASTED CHIPS WITH OLIVE OIL AND FRESH ROSEMARY

Patatine al forno con olio d'oliva e rosmarino

SERVES 6

650g Maris Piper
  potatoes, scrubbed
200ml extra virgin
  olive oil
1 tablespoon coarse
  sea salt
3 tablespoons chopped
  fresh rosemary

Place a bowl of these on the table and watch the hands descend. My kids usually make me cook a double batch just to make sure there's enough for the three of them. Best of all, they never ask me for ketchup as they love the flavour of the fresh rosemary. Serve to both children and adults with pretty much anything.

1. Preheat the oven to 200°C/gas mark 6. Cut the potatoes lengthways into 1cm-thick slices, then each slice into 2cm-thick chips.

2. Rinse under cold running water and pat dry with kitchen paper. Put the chips in a large roasting tin and spread out in a single layer. If your dish is not large enough, use 2 dishes.

3. Pour over the oil and sprinkle over the salt and rosemary. Toss together to combine. Bake for 45 minutes, turning over 3 or 4 times. When done, the chips will be golden and crisp on the outside and fluffy in the centre.

BAKED POLENTA

Polenta al forno

SERVES 6

1.75 litres vegetable
  stock
300g quick-cook
  polenta
½ teaspoon white
  pepper
Salted butter for
  greasing

Made from cornmeal, polenta has been a staple food all over northern Italy since the 18th century, and more recently its popularity has spread southwards to central Italy. In Lombardy and Piedmont the maize is ground quite coarsely, while in Veneto and central Italy it has a finer texture. Here I have baked the polenta, but it can also be simply boiled, grilled or fried. It's the perfect complement to meat, fish and vegetable dishes.

1. Preheat the oven to 190°C/gas mark 5. Pour the stock into a medium saucepan and bring to the boil over a high heat. Reduce the heat to low and gradually add the polenta, whisking continuously to prevent lumps from forming.

2. When all the polenta has been added, stir in the pepper and cook for a further 8 minutes or until the polenta starts to thicken, stirring all the time. Taste for seasoning.

3. Grease a round baking dish, 22cm diameter, with butter. Spoon the polenta into the dish. Transfer to the oven and bake for 20–25 minutes or until golden and set. Serve immediately.

BAKED MUSHROOMS STUFFED WITH GORGONZOLA AND PECORINO

Funghi al forno ripieni di Gorgonzola e pecorino

SERVES 6

6 large Portobello mushrooms

2 tablespoons fresh white breadcrumbs

1 garlic clove, peeled and chopped

4 tablespoons chopped fresh flat-leaf parsley

2 tablespoons freshly grated pecorino cheese

70g Gorgonzola dolce cheese, cut into small cubes

5 tablespoons extra virgin olive oil, plus extra for greasing

Portobello mushrooms have a robust, meaty texture making them excellent for roasting, baking and stuffing. Available year round, they are simply the larger, more mature form of the common cultivated white or chestnut mushroom. I've used Gorgonzola dolce here – a sweeter, milder version of Gorgonzola from Lombardy and Piedmont – but any blue cheese would be fine, and Parmesan is the best substitute for pecorino. Serve with a crisp green salad for a light lunch or with grilled fish.

1. Preheat the oven to 180°C/gas mark 4. Wipe the mushrooms clean with a cloth. Cut off and finely chop the stalks. Put them in a bowl and add the breadcrumbs, garlic, parsley, pecorino and Gorgonzola. Mix well to combine.

2. Brush a little oil on the bottom of a baking sheet and arrange the mushrooms on it. Spoon the stuffing into the mushroom caps, gently packing the mixture down with the back of a spoon.

3. Drizzle over the oil and bake for 15 minutes or until the crumbs are golden.

CANNELLINI BEAN AND CHERRY TOMATO SALAD WITH LEMON AND SAGE

Insalata di cannellini e pomodorini al limone e salvia

SERVES 6

300g dried cannellini beans
6 garlic cloves, peeled and left whole
20 fresh sage leaves
1 unwaxed lemon
150g fresh red cherry tomatoes, halved
150g fresh yellow cherry tomatoes, halved
2 tablespoons white wine vinegar
6 tablespoons extra virgin olive oil
3 tablespoons chopped fresh flat-leaf parsley
Salt and white pepper

Cannellini beans, which originate in Tuscany, are ideal for salads and are often paired with sage. This recipe is perfect for vegetarians, but I sometimes stir through some tinned tuna for a more substantial, healthy lunch. Add salt after cooking – never before, as it will give the beans a tough skin. You can use tinned cannellini beans as a shortcut, provided you rinse and drain them first.

1. Put the beans in a large bowl and pour over 1.5 litres of cold water. Leave to soak for about 12 hours.

2. Drain and rinse the beans thoroughly. Place them in a medium saucepan, cover with 1.5 litres of cold water and add the garlic and sage. Bring to the boil and boil rapidly for 10 minutes. Reduce the heat to low, cover and simmer gently for about 1½ hours or until the beans have softened but remain slightly firm. Drain and rinse under cold running water. Discard the garlic and sage.

3. Using a vegetable peeler, remove the zest from the lemon (leaving behind the bitter white pith) then cut the strips into fine shreds. Put the shreds in a large bowl and add the tomatoes and drained beans.

4. To make the dressing, squeeze the lemon and put the juice into a bowl with the vinegar. Gradually add the oil, whisking continuously. Stir in the parsley and season with salt and pepper. Pour the dressing over the vegetables and toss together to combine.

LENTIL AND SQUASH SALAD WITH WALNUTS AND CRANBERRIES

Insalata di lenticchie e zucca con noci e mirtilli rossi americani

SERVES 4

400g butternut squash, cut into 1cm cubes

2 tablespoons olive oil

400g dried green lentils

Grated zest and juice of 2 lemons

6 tablespoons extra virgin olive oil

3 spring onions, thinly sliced

1 cucumber, peeled, deseeded and diced

75g walnut pieces

50g dried cranberries, finely chopped

3 tablespoons chopped fresh flat-leaf parsley

Sea salt and freshly ground black pepper

Umbrian lentils are thought to be the best in Italy, with those from Abruzzo coming a close second. When I visited Umbria I met a farmer named Ettore, who has made it his mission to cultivate organic lentils using traditional methods. He showed me the old machine he uses for sorting and cleaning the pulses – the same one he used as a child. For lunch I made a salad from his beautiful lentils, combining them with roasted butternut squash, locally grown walnuts, cranberries and other ingredients – it's a really exciting mixture of contrasting flavours, colours and textures. Please try it!

1. Preheat the oven to 180°C/gas mark 4. Put the squash in a large roasting tin, drizzle with the olive oil and season with salt and pepper. Roast for 25–30 minutes or until soft and slightly golden then leave to cool.

2. Bring a large pan of salted water to the boil over a high heat. Add the lentils and cook for about 18–20 minutes or until tender, stirring occasionally. Drain well and leave to cool.

3. Meanwhile, to make the dressing, put the lemon juice in a small bowl. Slowly add the extra virgin olive oil, whisking constantly, until combined. Add some sea salt and pepper.

4. Place the lentils and squash in a large bowl and add the lemon zest, spring onions, cucumber, walnuts, cranberries and parsley. Pour the dressing over the salad and toss well. Serve at room temperature.

AUBERGINE SALAD WITH CHARGRILLED CHILLI, CAPERS AND FRESH HERBS

Insalata di melanzane con peperoncini grigliati

SERVES 4

50ml extra virgin olive oil, plus extra for greasing
4 aubergines (about 1kg in total), halved lengthways
1 fresh medium-hot red chilli
Juice of ½ lemon
1 tablespoon capers, drained
1 teaspoon salt
2 tablespoons shredded fresh mint
2 tablespoons chopped fresh flat-leaf parsley

Aubergines arrived in the Mediterranean region with the Arabs in the Middle Ages and they soon spread throughout southern Italy. However, it was not until the 20th century that they became popular in central and northern regions. This spicy, piquant aubergine salad is the perfect accompaniment to fish and meat. Serve with warm, crusty bread.

1. Preheat the oven to 180°C/gas mark 4. Brush oil over the bottom of a large baking sheet and lay on the aubergines, cut-side up. Roast for 45 minutes or until softened.

2. Remove the aubergines from the oven and scoop the flesh into a colander set over a bowl to catch the liquid. Discard the skins and leave the flesh to cool and drain thoroughly.

3. Preheat a ridged cast-iron chargrill pan over a high heat for 5–10 minutes. Place the chilli in the pan and grill for 2 minutes each side until lightly charred. Cut the chilli into large pieces and set aside.

4. To make the dressing, measure 50ml of the aubergine liquid and discard the rest. Pour the liquid into a small bowl and add the lemon juice, capers and salt. Gradually whisk in the oil.

5. Chop the aubergine into bite-sized pieces and arrange on a serving platter. Pour over the dressing and garnish with the reserved chilli, mint and parsley. Serve immediately, or leave to rest for 1 hour and serve at room temperature.

SPELT AND MIXED-LEAF SALAD WITH TOMATOES, OLIVES AND COURGETTES

Insalatona di foglie miste con farro, pomodori, olive e zucchine

SERVES 4-6

250g pearled spelt
25 fresh yellow baby
  plum tomatoes,
  quartered
200g pitted green
  olives, drained and
  halved lengthways
1 small courgette, finely
  diced
Grated zest of 1
  unwaxed lemon
1 head of red radicchio,
  cut into 1cm-thick
  strips
100g frisée, cut into
  1cm-thick strips
6 tablespoons extra
  virgin olive oil
4 tablespoons balsamic
  vinegar
Salt and freshly ground
  black pepper

Spelt is an ancient cereal grain and a healthy, fibre-rich alternative to rice. Here it is combined with tender red radicchio (a delicacy of Veneto, with a bitter yet refined flavour) and feathery green frisée to produce the most spectacular-looking salad, ideal for serving with barbecued fish or meat.

1. Place the spelt in a fine-meshed sieve and rinse well under cold running water. Tip it into a small saucepan, cover with cold water and add 1 teaspoon of salt.

2. Place the pan over a high heat and bring to the boil then stir. Reduce the heat to medium, cover and simmer for 15-20 minutes or until tender. Drain thoroughly and leave to cool completely.

3. Combine the spelt, tomatoes, olives, courgette, lemon zest, radicchio and frisée leaves. Pour over the oil and vinegar and season with salt and pepper. Toss together and transfer to a serving platter.

Many people avoid baking, believing it to be too difficult or labour-intensive to bother with – but not so, my friends! There are some pizzas, pies and breads in this chapter that are so easy to prepare you'll be amazed, and the satisfaction of baking your own more than makes up for any extra time you have spent in the kitchen.

PIZZA, PIES & BREADS

PIZZA TOPPED WITH SMOKED PANCETTA, PEPPERS AND FONTINA

Pizza bianca con pancetta affumicata e peperoni

MAKES 2

200g strong white flour, plus extra for dusting

1 x 7g sachet fast-action (easy blend) dried yeast

¾ teaspoon salt

2 tablespoons extra virgin olive oil, plus extra for greasing

For the topping

5 tablespoons extra virgin olive oil, plus extra for drizzling

2 yellow peppers, deseeded and thinly sliced

1 orange pepper, deseeded and thinly sliced

175g fontina cheese, rind removed and cut into cubes

12 slices of smoked pancetta

Salt and freshly ground black pepper

Pizza is a southern Italian speciality, but in recent decades it has become increasingly popular all over northern Italy. As a Neapolitan I was rather disappointed to see that many pizzerias in the north often use electric ovens rather than the traditional wood-fired ovens used in the south, but I was pleased to see that they are experimental with their toppings. I really liked this one from the Trentino-Alto Adige region, using the local fontina cheese rather than the more usual mozzarella.

1. Combine the flour, yeast and salt in a large bowl. Make a well in the centre and add the oil, then gradually pour in 140ml of warm water and mix together using the handle of a wooden spoon to create a wet dough.

2. Knead the dough on a lightly floured surface for about 5 minutes or until soft, smooth and elastic. Shape the dough into a round and place in a large oiled bowl. Brush the top with a little oil and cover with cling film. Leave to rest at room temperature for 20 minutes.

3. Meanwhile, make the topping. Heat the oil in a medium frying pan over a medium heat. Add the peppers, season with salt and pepper and fry for 10 minutes, stirring occasionally. Set aside to cool. Preheat the oven to 220°C/ gas mark 7.

4. Brush 2 baking sheets with oil. Turn out the dough onto a lightly floured surface and knead just 3 or 4 times to knock out the air. Halve the dough and roll out 1 half directly onto one of the baking sheets, rolling and stretching the dough to make a round about 25cm diameter and 1–2cm thick. Make a small rim by pulling up the edge slightly. Repeat with the remaining piece of dough.

5. Scatter the cooled peppers and fontina evenly over the pizza bases, avoiding the rim, and season with salt and pepper. Lay the sliced pancetta on top and drizzle over a little extra oil. Bake for about 12–14 minutes or until golden brown.

Pizza del Lago di Como

MAKES 1 (SERVES 2)

200g strong white
   flour, plus extra for
   dusting
1 x 7g sachet fast-action
   (easy blend) dried
   yeast
¾ teaspoon salt
2 tablespoons extra
   virgin olive oil, plus
   extra for greasing

For the filling
3 tablespoons ricotta
   cheese, drained
Large handful (about
   40g) of rocket leaves
75g fontina cheese,
   rind removed and
   sliced
50g semi-dried
   tomatoes in oil,
   drained
50g pitted black
   olives (preferably
   Taggiasca), drained
   and halved
Salt and freshly ground
   black pepper

When filming around Lake Como the TV crew and I went to a local pizzeria for dinner. The owner told us that this stuffed pizza is George Clooney's favourite – so of course we had to try it. I can tell you it was delicious, and if it's good enough for George it's surely good enough for us. Here is my own version of it for you to try. *Buon appetito!*

1. Combine the flour, yeast and salt in a large bowl. Make a well in the centre and add the oil, then gradually pour in 140ml of warm water and mix together using the handle of a wooden spoon to create a wet dough.

2. Knead the dough on a lightly floured surface for about 5 minutes or until soft, smooth and elastic. Shape the dough into a round and place in a large oiled bowl. Brush the top with a little oil and cover with cling film. Leave to rest at room temperature for 20 minutes. Preheat the oven to 220°C/gas mark 7.

3. Brush a baking sheet with oil and line it with baking parchment. Turn out the dough onto a lightly floured surface and knead just 3 or 4 times to knock out the air. Halve the dough and roll out 1 piece directly onto the baking sheet, rolling and stretching the dough to make a round about 20cm diameter.

4. To make the filling, top the pizza base with the ricotta, using the back of a tablespoon to spread it over the surface and leaving a small border of about 1cm all round. Season with salt and pepper. Scatter over the rocket then the fontina, semi-dried tomatoes and olives.

5. Roll out the second piece of dough to the same size as the first and gently lay it on top of the filling. Bring the edges together to enclose and press firmly to seal. Fold in the edge and crimp with your fingers, as you would a pie, to create a thick edge with a decorative finish. Brush the surface with oil.

6. Bake for about 16 minutes or until the crust is golden brown. Cut into wedges and serve immediately.

FONTINA AND PARMA HAM PARCELS

Fagottini con fontina e prosciutto crudo

SERVES 6

300g shop-bought
  puff pastry
Plain flour for dusting
12 slices of Parma ham
450g fontina cheese,
  rind removed and cut
  into 12 slices
18 semi-dried tomatoes
  in oil, drained
1 egg yolk
1 teaspoon milk
Salt and freshly ground
  black pepper

These are amazing baked sandwiches to eat at home or take with you to the office or on a picnic. You can substitute the fontina with any melting cheese and use salami or cooked ham instead of Parma ham – the possibilities are endless. Serve with rocket tossed in olive oil and balsamic vinegar and a bottle of cold beer.

1. Preheat the oven to 190°C/gas mark 5. Roll out the pastry on a lightly floured work surface until it is about the thickness of a £1 coin. Slice into 6 smaller rectangles.

2. Lay a slice of ham on 1 half of a pastry rectangle, leaving a small border of about 1cm. Place a slice of fontina on top, then arrange 3 of the semi-dried tomatoes on top of the cheese. Cover the tomatoes with another slice of ham and cheese.

3. Combine the egg yolk and milk in a small bowl. Brush a little of the egg mixture around the border. Fold over to enclose the filling and press all around the edge to seal. To secure the seal, press the tines of a fork round the pastry edge. Repeat for all the parcels.

4. Line a large baking sheet with baking parchment and lay the parcels on it, spacing them well apart. Brush more of the egg mixture over each parcel to glaze (you may not need it all). Bake for 18 minutes or until golden. Serve immediately.

Pastiera di pollo

SERVES 8

4 tablespoons plain
flour, plus extra for
dusting

1kg skinless, boneless
chicken thighs, each
cut into 4 pieces

7 tablespoons olive oil,
plus extra for greasing

2 large red onions,
peeled and finely
sliced

2 tablespoons caster
sugar

1 red pepper, deseeded
and finely sliced

1 leek, cut in half
lengthways and finely
sliced

1 courgette, cut in half
lengthways and sliced

1 tablespoon fresh
thyme leaves

2 large eggs

100ml double cream

100g freshly grated
Grana Padano cheese

Grated zest of 1
unwaxed lemon

400g shop-bought puff
pastry

Salt and white pepper

I first tasted this pie in the city of Pisa, Tuscany. I loved its simplicity and the sweet flavour of the caramelised onions – it's definitely one I will do over and over again. If you want a bit more of a 'kick', replace the Grana Padano with Gorgonzola. Serve with a side salad.

1. Put the flour on a large plate and season with salt and pepper. Dust the chicken with the seasoned flour. Heat half the oil in a large frying pan over a medium to high heat. When very hot, add half the chicken and fry for about 5 minutes each side or until golden brown all over. Transfer to a large plate using a slotted spoon and set aside. Repeat for the remaining chicken.

2. Pour in the remaining oil and reduce the heat. Add the onions and sugar and fry very gently for 10 minutes, stirring only occasionally so the onions can caramelise. Add the red pepper, leek and courgette, sprinkle over the thyme and season with salt and pepper. Fry for 15 minutes or until softened, stirring occasionally. Take off the heat and leave to cool.

3. Preheat the oven to 180°C/gas mark 4. Break one of the eggs into a medium bowl and beat lightly with a fork. Pour in the cream then stir in the Grana Padano and lemon zest. Season with salt and pepper and set aside. Grease a loose-bottomed flan tin, 25cm diameter and ideally fluted.

4. On a lightly floured work surface, roll out two thirds of the pastry and use it to line the tin. Trim any excess. Tip in the cooled vegetables and arrange the chicken on top. Pour over the egg mixture. Beat the remaining egg in a bowl and brush it around the edge of the pastry.

5. To make the lid, roll out the remaining pastry slightly larger than the size of the tin and lay it over the filling. Trim if necessary. Pinch the edges together to secure. Brush more of the beaten egg over the pie to glaze (you may not need it all). Cut a small slit in the centre of the lid to allow steam to escape.

6. Bake for 30 minutes or until the pastry is risen and golden brown. Take out of the oven and leave to rest for 5 minutes. Remove the pie from its tin then slice. Serve warm.

PANE & PANIFICI

Any visitor to Italy will know that moments after you sit down at a restaurant table a basket of bread (*pane*) will be placed before you. Indeed, a meal without bread is unthinkable to an Italian. Bread has been the mainstay of our diet for thousands of years and it is at the centre of family, social and religious life. It is considered almost sacred by some – loaves may have the mark of a cross cut into them before they're baked, and to throw bread away is considered by many to be a sin or to bring bad luck. Certainly, stale bread is very rarely wasted – we put it into salads and soups, and turn it into breadcrumbs to use in many dishes.

The ancient Greeks invented the large wood-burning oven for breadmaking, and the Romans were the first to refine milling practices to produce white bread. They also enriched loaves by adding eggs, milk and butter – but only for the wealthy few. Today most breads in Italy are still baked in traditional brick ovens and there are well over 350 different types in over a thousand shapes and sizes, ranging from small rolls to vast loaves intended to last a family for a week. Wherever you go in Italy you will see *panifici* (bakeries) everywhere – their shelves stacked high with beautiful bread all freshly baked on the premises.

Every region has its own traditional breads, differing in shape and the type of flour used. Many contain seeds or grains for added flavour and texture.

Buckwheat bread Popular in northern Italy, particularly Lombardy and Val d'Aosta. Buckwheat (*grano saraceno*) flour, which dates from the time when wheat was not yet cultivated in Italy, has an earthy flavour and is sometimes used to make gluten-free loaves.

Crescentina Bread from Emilia-Romagna made with lard. It is usually cut into small shapes and fried, then eaten with cheese and cured meats.

Ciabatta A relatively modern shape of bread, ciabatta (which means 'slipper') has a thin crust and light, airy texture.

Ciambella A ring-shaped white bread with a crusty exterior, from central and southern Italy.

Focaccia Resembling a thick pizza, focaccia comes in many different forms and flavourings throughout Italy,

including sweet versions. Liguria offers the greatest variety. In Tuscany the equivalent is known as schiacciata.

Grissini Breadsticks are a speciality from Piedmont but have now spread throughout Italy.

Michetta Also known as rosetta ('little rose') because of its shape, this is a light white bread roll from Lombardy.

Piadina A thin, soft flatbread from Emilia-Romagna, usually eaten with salami or prosciutto.

Pumpernickel A slightly sour, heavy-textured, German-style black bread from Trentino-Alto Adige.

Rye bread Slightly lighter than the rye bread of northern and eastern Europe, this is popular in the Val d'Aosta and Trentino-Alto Adige.

Ciambella di pane con olive Taggiasca

MAKES 1 LOAF

680g strong white
  flour, plus extra for
  dusting
10g fast-action (easy
  blend) dried yeast
2 teaspoons salt
Extra virgin olive oil for
  greasing and brushing
200g pitted Taggiasca
  olives, drained and
  roughly chopped

A speciality of Liguria, Taggiasca olives are small and deep red in colour and have a sweet, mild, fruity flavour. They are excellent in bread and transform a plain white loaf into something really special. When mixing the dough it's better to have it on the moist side. If the mixture sticks to your hands it's a good sign.

1. Combine the flour, yeast and salt in a large bowl. Make a well in the centre and pour in 400ml of warm water in a steady stream. Using a round-bladed knife, mix to a soft dough. Add a little more water or extra flour if needed.

2. Gather the dough and knead on a lightly floured surface for 8–10 minutes or until smooth and elastic. Shape into a round and place in a large oiled bowl. Cover with cling film and leave in a warm place for 1–1½ hours or until doubled in size. Grease a large baking sheet with oil.

3. Return the dough to the floured work surface, sprinkle over the olives and knead until combined.

4. Using a sharp knife, cut off one-third of the dough. Shape it into a ball. Shape the larger piece of dough into a ball and place it on the baking sheet. Gently flatten the larger ball slightly and, using a sharp knife, cut a 5cm cross in the centre. Brush with a little water and place the smaller ball on top. Push a floured wooden spoon handle right through the centre of both balls.

5. Cover lightly with a tea towel and leave to rise in a warm place for about 40–45 minutes or until doubled in size. Meanwhile, preheat the oven to 220°C/gas mark 7.

6. Brush a little oil over the loaf. Bake for 40 minutes or until golden and firm. It should sound hollow when tapped on the underside. Transfer to a wire rack to cool and serve warm.

LIGURIAN POTATO BREAD

Pagnotta Ligure alle patate

MAKES 1 LOAF

250g floury potatoes, such as Desirée or Maris Piper, peeled and quartered
350g strong white flour, plus extra for dusting
100g wholemeal flour, plus extra for sprinkling
1 x 7g sachet fast-action (easy blend) dried yeast
1 tablespoon fresh thyme leaves
2 teaspoons salt
30g salted butter, melted
Extra virgin olive oil for greasing and brushing

Liguria is famous for its potato dishes. Potato bread was once a staple in its mountain areas, popular because it was both flavoursome and remained soft for longer than bread made from regular wheat flour – an important factor when bread-baking took place only once a week or fortnight. In the mid-1960s commercially made potato bread was banned, as the government associated it with poverty and backwardness, but the ban was lifted and it has recently made a comeback, featuring in many of the potato festivals (*Sagre di patate*) held in Italy each year.

1. Place the potatoes in a medium saucepan, cover with cold water and add some salt. Bring to the boil and simmer for 15-20 minutes or until tender. Drain well and leave for 2-3 minutes then pass through a potato ricer set over a bowl or mash using a potato masher until really smooth. Set aside to cool.

2. Combine the flours, yeast, thyme and salt in a large bowl. Make a well in the centre. Pour in 150ml of warm water then the melted butter. Use a round-bladed knife to mix. Add the mashed potatoes and mix well using the handle of a wooden spoon to create a soft dough.

3. Gather the dough and knead on a lightly floured surface for 8-10 minutes or until smooth and elastic. Shape into a round and place in a large oiled bowl. Cover with cling film and leave in a warm place for about 1-1½ hours or until doubled in size. Grease a large baking sheet with oil.

4. Return the dough to the floured work surface and knead 3 or 4 times. Form the dough into an oval and place on the oiled baking sheet. Cover lightly with a tea towel and leave to rise in a warm place for 40-50 minutes or until doubled in size. Meanwhile, preheat the oven to 220°C/gas mark 7.

5. Make diagonal cuts in the top of the loaf to create a criss-cross effect. Brush the surface with a little oil and sprinkle over some wholemeal flour. Bake for 30 minutes. To test if the bread is cooked through, tap the bottom of the loaf: it should sound hollow. Transfer to a wire rack to cool and serve warm.

Focaccia farcita con Taleggio e noci

SERVES 4-6

350g strong white flour, plus extra for dusting

5g fast-action (easy blend) dried yeast

1 teaspoon salt

6 tablespoons extra virgin olive oil, plus extra for greasing and brushing

For the filling

300g Taleggio cheese, rind removed and cut into small cubes

100g walnut halves, roughly chopped

2 garlic cloves, peeled and finely sliced

Freshly ground black pepper

In my restaurants we make a stuffed focaccia using mozzarella and fresh basil and our customers absolutely love it, so I decided to create another version with a northern Italian twist. Here I've used Taleggio (an Alpine cheese from Lombardy) and walnuts, which makes a wonderful change. If you prefer, use hazelnuts or pine nuts instead of walnuts.

1. Place the flour in a large bowl. Add the yeast and salt and mix well. Make a well in the centre and add 3 tablespoons of the oil then gradually pour in 200ml of warm water and mix together using the handle of a wooden spoon.

2. Knead the dough on a lightly floured surface for 8-10 minutes or until smooth and elastic, adding a little more flour if it's really sticky. Shape the dough into a round and place in a large, oiled bowl. Cover with cling film and leave in a warm place for about 1 hour or until doubled in size. Brush a large baking sheet with a little oil and set aside.

3. Turn out the dough onto a lightly floured surface and knead just 3 or 4 times. Using your fingertips, gently push the dough to a rectangle about 30 x 25cm. Cover lightly with a tea towel and leave to rise for 8-10 minutes.

4. Scatter the Taleggio, walnuts and garlic over the dough, leaving a small border of about 1cm all round. Grind over plenty of black pepper.

5. Starting from one of the shorter sides, tightly roll up the dough like a Swiss roll. Press together the side edges and tuck under under to seal. Ensure the join is underneath then transfer to the oiled baking sheet. Cover again with the tea towel and leave to rise in a warm place for 30-40 minutes or until doubled in size. Meanwhile, preheat the oven to 200°C/gas mark 6.

6. Brush the focaccia with the remaining 3 tablespoons of oil and prick holes all over with a skewer. Bake for 35 minutes or until golden. Transfer to a wire rack to cool slightly, then slice and serve warm.

Desserts are incredible in northern Italy – rich, creamy puddings, ice creams and semi-freddos, cakes, biscuits and pastries such as strudel – they are all absolutely irresistible. Many desserts from the north feature nuts – for instance, hazelnuts are very popular in Piedmont, where they are cultivated – and chocolate is a favourite wherever you go.

DESSERTS

COFFEE GRANITA WITH AMARETTO   193

Granita al caffè con liquore all'amaretto

SERVES 10

75g caster sugar
500ml freshly made
  hot espresso
3 tablespoons amaretto
  (almond liqueur)

I've never met an Italian who doesn't drink coffee, and coffee-flavoured desserts are a firm favourite in Italy. Granitas are really a Sicilian speciality, but they've spread throughout Italy and on a hot day they're so much more refreshing than ice cream. If you don't have an espresso machine, add ground espresso coffee to a pan of hot water, bring it to the boil and leave to infuse for 5 minutes, then strain.

1. Stir the sugar into the hot espresso until it dissolves. Add the amaretto and pour the mixture into a 1-litre shallow, freezerproof container. Leave to cool completely. Cover and transfer to the freezer for about 4 hours or until ice starts to freeze around the edges.

2. Whisk the granita with a fork to break up the ice crystals and return to the freezer. Repeat the process every 20 minutes over the next 2 hours or until there is no liquid left in the container and the mixture just consists of broken-up ice crystals.

3. Rinse each glass with cold water (inside and out) and place in the freezer for 2 minutes. Take the granita out of the freezer 2 minutes before serving to soften slightly. Spoon into the frosted glasses and serve immediately.

DESSERTS

EASY SOUR CHERRY ICE CREAM WITH AMARETTO SAUCE

Gelato facile all'amarena

SERVES 6

120g dried sweetened
 sour cherries
600ml double cream
175ml sweetened
 condensed milk
1 teaspoon vanilla
 extract

For the sauce
3 tablespoons cherry
 jam
1 tablespoon amaretto
 (almond liqueur)

Sour cherries (also known as tart cherries) are smaller and softer than sweet cherries. Although they are sometimes eaten fresh, in Italy – where Morello is the most popular variety – sour cherries are usually used in jams, jellies, sorbets and ice creams. This particular ice cream contains condensed milk, which gives a creamy, smooth texture without churning – a bit of a cheat, but no one need ever know!

1. Put half the cherries in a blender, add 100ml of the cream and blitz to make a purée. Set aside.

2. Put the remaining cream, the condensed milk and vanilla extract in a medium bowl and beat using an electric hand whisk for about 3 minutes or until quite stiff. Stir in the cherry purée and the remaining cherries.

3. Spoon the mixture into a 1-litre shallow, freezerproof container. Cover and transfer to the freezer overnight or until solid.

4. Take the container out of the freezer 10 minutes before serving. Gently heat the jam and amaretto. Scoop the ice cream into bowls and top with the sauce.

CHOCOLATE AND HAZELNUT SEMI-FREDDO WITH HOT CHOCOLATE SAUCE

Semifreddo alla Nutella con cioccolato fondente caldo

SERVES 8

10 egg yolks
150g caster sugar
300g hazelnut
 chocolate spread
 (Nutella)
500ml double cream
40g roasted chopped
 hazelnuts, plus extra
 to decorate

For the sauce
250g dark chocolate
300ml double cream

Italy is the world's second largest producer of hazelnuts after Turkey, and Piedmont – home of the famous hazelnut chocolate spread Nutella (see the recipe introduction on page 208) – is the main hazelnut-growing area in Italy. Like the Piedmontese, I love the combination of hazelnuts and chocolate so have created this semi-frozen dessert for you. It has a soft, velvety texture and – unlike ice cream – semi-freddo (meaning 'half cold') never freezes to a solid block and can be cut into slices to serve. The hot chocolate sauce isn't necessary – but how can you resist?

1. Dampen the bottom and sides of a 1kg loaf tin using a pastry brush dipped in water then line the tin with cling film. Set aside.

2. Put the egg yolks and sugar in a medium heatproof bowl and set the bowl over a pan of gently simmering water. The base of the bowl should not touch the water. Stir with a balloon whisk for about 5 minutes until the sugar has dissolved and the mixture is thick and creamy. Remove from the heat, stir in the hazelnut chocolate spread and leave to cool completely.

3. Place the cream in a large bowl and whip until thick enough to just hold its shape and form soft peaks. Gently fold the cream into the cooled hazelnut mixture in 3 batches then fold in the nuts.

4. Tip the mixture into the prepared tin. Cover with cling film and freeze for 8 hours or overnight until set.

5. Remove the tin from the freezer 10 minutes before serving. Meanwhile, make the chocolate sauce. Break the chocolate into a large heatproof bowl, add the cream and set the bowl over a pan of gently simmering water. The base of the bowl should not touch the water. Heat until the chocolate has melted.

6. Scoop the semi-freddo into bowls or cut into slices. Pour over the hot chocolate sauce and sprinkle with chopped hazelnuts.

GELATI & GELATERIE

We Italians pride ourselves on our amazing ice cream, and it's becoming increasingly popular – what was once a summer speciality is now enjoyed all year round. We eat it any time of day, but particularly after dinner, when taking a *passeggiata* – our traditional evening stroll around the town with family and friends. Perhaps unsurprisingly, Italy has the highest number of artisan ice cream parlours (*gelaterie*) in Europe, which has as many as the rest of the world put together.

Ice cream originally came from China then moved across India and the Middle East before arriving in southern Italy with the Arabs. So although Italy wasn't responsible for inventing ice cream, it certainly played a large part in its development and was responsible for introducing it to Europe and later to the rest of the world.

When the Arabs ruled Sicily in the 9th and 10th centuries, they would use fruit juices and mountain snow to make *sharbat* – a frozen drink that resembled the modern *granita*. With improvements in freezing techniques, this evolved into the first *sorbetto*, or water ice, by the 16th century. Eggs and cream were added in the 17th century – a Sicilian inventor created a machine that homogenised the mixture of egg custard, fruit juices, sugar, and ice – and modern ice cream as we know it was born. By the 19th century Italian *gelati* and the ice cream man with his cart had become popular around the world.

The Italian word *gelato* (literally 'frozen') can be confusing. It is used generally for ice cream and sorbets, although true Italian *gelato* differs from other ice cream in several ways, and sorbets are quite different (see below).

There are four main types of frozen dessert in Italy. Generally, northern Italians tend to prefer richer, dairy-based ice creams made with eggs, while southerners usually opt for lighter, egg-free sorbets and granitas.

Gelato True Italian gelato is a mixture of egg custard, sugar and flavourings. It is made with milk (sometimes skimmed) rather than cream, as is often the case with ordinary ice cream, so it has a lower fat content (usually about 4–5.5 per cent butterfat rather than 10 per cent or more). There are strict rules about its production – no more than 2 per cent of additives are allowed, and the sweetness must be provided by natural rather than synthetic sugars. It has less air whipped into it than ice cream, and is stored a few degrees warmer, so it has more flavour, greater density, and a softer, silkier texture.

Granita Originating in Sicily, granitas are a frozen dessert or drink made from coarse grated ice, sugar and flavourings – often fruit juices. (See also page 193.)

Semi-freddo Meaning 'half cold', this is a semi-frozen, mousse-like type of ice cream made with eggs, whipped cream, sugar and flavouring. It isn't churned like ice cream or gelato and is sometimes cut into slices. (See also page 196.)

Sorbetto A water ice flavoured with fruit purées, sorbet does not contain dairy or eggs.

Musse deliziosa di cioccolato fondente e frutti di bosco

SERVES 6-8

180g plain dark chocolate
60g unsalted butter
Pinch of salt
5 large eggs, separated
50g light brown muscovado sugar
½ teaspoon ground cinnamon
Blueberries to decorate
Raspberries to decorate
Shelled pistachio nuts, chopped, to decorate

Some of the best chocolate in Italy comes from the northern city of Turin, the capital of Piedmont, where chocolate-making has been established since the late 18th century. At this time, Italy exported its chocolate to France, Germany, Austria and Switzerland; indeed, it was the famous Turin-based firm Caffarel that inspired the Swiss to start making chocolate on a commercial scale. Rich chocolate desserts are popular in the region, and being close to the French border one of the favourites is chocolate mousse. For variety, you could add a couple of tablespoons of espresso coffee to make it a mocha chocolate mousse.

1. Break the chocolate into a large heatproof bowl, add the butter and salt and set the bowl over a pan of gently simmering water. The base of the bowl should not touch the water. Leave until just melted then remove the pan from the heat, stir and leave the chocolate to cool slightly.

2. Add the egg yolks one at a time, whisking continually, then stir in the sugar and cinnamon. Set aside.

3. Place the egg whites in a medium bowl and whisk with an electric hand whisk on full speed until they form stiff peaks. Using a metal spoon, gently fold one third of the egg whites into the cooled chocolate mixture until well blended. Fold in the remaining egg whites in 2 stages.

4. Spoon the mixture into individual glasses, cover with cling film and refrigerate for at least 5 hours or until set.

5. Decorate each mousse with the blueberries and raspberries. Sieve the pistachios to remove the dusty skins and sprinkle them over the top.

NO-BAKE APPLE, RAISIN AND AMARETTO STRUDEL WITH RASPBERRY SAUCE

Sfogliatine fritte alle mele, uva passa e amaretto con salsa di lamponi

MAKES 4

3 Golden Delicious apples, cored, peeled and cut into 5mm cubes

300g unsalted butter

3 tablespoons Demerara sugar

50ml amaretto (almond liqueur)

100g plump raisins

1 x 270g packet of shop-bought filo pastry (6 large sheets)

150g raspberries

½ teaspoon ground cinnamon

50g icing sugar

In Trentino-Alto Adige many fantastic Austrian-style desserts are available, my favourite probably being apple strudel. When I visited the stunning lake at Castillo Toblino I felt inspired to make strudel but didn't have access to an oven, so I created this no-bake recipe. I think it works just as well as the traditional version and the raspberry sauce makes it extra special.

1. To make the filling put the apples and 50g of the butter in a large frying pan over a low to medium heat. Once the butter has melted stir in the sugar. As the sugar starts to dissolve add the amaretto then the raisins. Cook gently for 15–20 minutes or until the apples are softened, stirring occasionally. Leave to cool.

2. In a small saucepan melt 100g of the butter over a low heat. Stack the filo pastry sheets on a board. Using a sharp knife, cut in half lengthways to make 12 long strips of filo measuring about 35 x 12cm. Cover the filo strips with a damp tea towel to prevent them from drying out. Take one strip of filo and brush with some of the melted butter. Place another strip on top and brush with butter. Repeat once more. You will have 3 layers of filo with melted butter between each layer and on top.

3. Place 2 rounded tablespoons of the filling at one end of the strip, 2cm in from the edge. Take the right corner and fold diagonally to the left, enclosing the filling and forming a triangle. Fold again along the upper crease of the triangle. Keep folding in this way until you reach the end of the strip, then fold over to seal. Brush all over with more butter. Place on a baking sheet and cover with a damp tea towel while you make the remaining strudel.

4. To make the sauce, purée the raspberries in a blender or food processor then push them through a sieve to remove the seeds. Combine the cinnamon and icing sugar in a small bowl. Set aside.

5. Melt the remaining butter in the frying pan over a low to medium heat. Add the strudel parcels and fry gently for about 3–4 minutes each side or until golden. Remove the parcels using a slotted spoon and drain on kitchen paper. Transfer the strudel parcels to serving plates. Sprinkle with the cinnamon sugar, drizzle with the sauce and serve immediately.

Ciambelline al limone e vino bianco

MAKES ABOUT 35

500g self-raising flour,
 plus extra for dusting
160g caster sugar, plus
 4 tablespoons for
 coating
1 teaspoon baking
 powder
Grated zest of 1
 unwaxed lemon
Pinch of salt
140ml dry white wine
100ml extra virgin olive
 oil

A speciality of northern Italy, these delicious biscuits are often served as an Easter treat. I have tried them with red wine and they work well too. If you have any biscuits left over, store them in an airtight container – they will last up to a week. Serve with a dessert wine.

1. Preheat the oven to 180°C/gas mark 4. Put the flour, sugar, baking powder, lemon zest and salt in a large bowl and lightly mix. Stir in the wine and oil using a wooden spoon until well combined.

2. Gather the dough and knead on a lightly floured surface for about 5 minutes or until smooth.

3. Break off small pieces of dough. Using the palms of your hands, roll each piece into a sausage shape about 6cm long and 2cm thick. Bring the ends together to make a ring shape. Press the ends together to seal. Repeat for the remaining biscuits.

4. Line 2 baking sheets with baking parchment. Put the 4 tablespoons of sugar on a plate and dip a dough ring in the sugar, coating one side only. Lay the ring, coated-side up, on one of the lined sheets. Repeat for the remaining biscuits, placing them 3cm apart and using both baking sheets.

5. Bake for 25 minutes or until golden. Remove from the oven and leave on the baking sheets for a few minutes, then transfer to a wire rack to cool.

POLENTA AND AMARETTO BISCUITS

Biscotti di mais e amaretto

MAKES ABOUT 60

120g sultanas
5 tablespoons amaretto
    (almond liqueur)
3 large egg yolks
110g caster sugar
160g plain flour, plus
    extra for dusting
160g fine polenta
½ teaspoon baking
    powder
150g salted butter,
    melted
Icing sugar for dusting

Dried ground polenta is widely used in baking in the north of Italy, where it's often added to pastry, cakes and biscuits to add flavour and texture, as you'll discover if you bake these lovely crunchy biscuits. If you're not a fan of almond flavour you can use a lemon-flavoured liqueur (limoncello) instead of amaretto. Serve with espresso.

1. Put the sultanas in a small bowl, pour over the amaretto and leave to soak for 1 hour. Drain and set aside.

2. Place the egg yolks and sugar in a large bowl and beat together using an electric whisk until pale and fluffy. Sift the flour, polenta and baking powder into the yolk mixture and add the melted butter gradually, stirring with a wooden spoon until combined. Fold in the sultanas.

3. Line 2 baking sheets with baking parchment. Lightly dust the work surface with flour. Cut the dough in half. Using the palms of your hands, roll out each piece to make 2 long 'ropes', about 4cm diameter. Place on one of the lined sheets and refrigerate for 1 hour. Meanwhile, preheat the oven to 180°C/ gas mark 4.

4. Cut across the dough 'ropes' to make 1cm-thick discs. Place them flat-side down and 3cm apart on the 2 lined sheets.

5. Bake for 15 minutes or until golden. Remove from the oven and leave on the baking sheets for a few minutes, then transfer to a wire rack to cool. Sift icing sugar over the top.

CHOCOLATE AND HAZELNUT BISCUITS

Biscotti con Nutella

MAKES ABOUT 16

3 hardboiled eggs (see page 22, step 1)

170g plain flour, plus extra for dusting

10g caster sugar

50g salted butter (room temperature)

2 tablespoons full-fat milk

1 teaspoon vanilla extract

75g hazelnut chocolate spread (Nutella)

2 tablespoons roasted chopped hazelnuts

You can use any hazelnut chocolate spread to make these delicious biscuits, but you will probably be most familiar with Nutella. Famous throughout the globe today, Nutella was created in Alba, Piedmont, just after World War II. It was the brainchild of the pastry-shop owner Pietro Ferrero, who wanted to create an inexpensive snack to eat with bread that would combine hazelnuts (which were abundant locally) with chocolate (which was rationed after the war). It was initially a solid block that needed slicing, but later became the spreadable Nutella – an instant success.

1. Peel the eggs and discard the whites. Place the yolks in a fine sieve set over a large bowl and press them through using the back of a spoon. Sift the flour and sugar over the egg yolks. Add the butter, milk and vanilla and beat thoroughly for about 3 minutes to create a smooth dough.

2. Line 2 baking sheets with baking parchment. Lightly dust the work surface with flour. Break off small pieces of dough and, using the palms of your hands, roll each piece into a small ball. Flatten the balls slightly then use your thumb to make an indentation in the centre of each ball. Place the balls on the lined sheets 3cm apart and refrigerate for 1 hour. Meanwhile, preheat the oven to 180°C/gas mark 4.

3. Bake for 15 minutes or until golden. Remove from the oven and leave on the baking sheets for a few minutes, then transfer to a wire rack to cool completely. To serve, fill each indentation with a teaspoon of Nutella then sprinkle over the hazelnuts.

UNSER EIS IST GARANTIERT NATÜRLICH OHNE ZUSÄTZLICHEN FARB-UND KUNSTSTOFFEN
OUR ICE-CREAM IS GUARANTEED NATURAL WITHOUT ANY ADDITIONAL COLOURS AND CHEMICAL INGREDIENTS

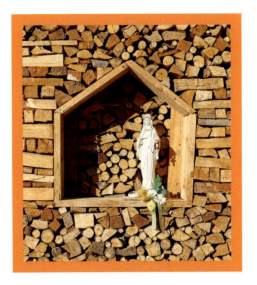

Torta di mele e rosmarino

SERVES 8

Butter (room
  temperature) for
  greasing
3 medium eggs
150g caster sugar
125g plain yogurt
120ml sunflower oil
1 teaspoon vanilla
  extract
230g self-raising flour
½ teaspoon ground
  cinnamon
1 tablespoon chopped
  fresh rosemary
2 red dessert apples
  (preferably Red Gala),
  quartered, peeled,
  cored and thinly
  sliced
2 tablespoons apricot
  jam

As I was filming in the region of Trentino-Alto Adige I discovered that many locals have their own secret recipe for the perfect apple cake. The film crew and I were constantly trying different recipes and this is the one we all agreed is the best. Thank you to chef Stefano from Ristorante Pellegrino for sharing his secret recipe with me – and now with you too.

1. Preheat the oven to 180°C/gas mark 4. Grease a deep, loose-bottomed round cake tin, 20cm diameter, and line with baking parchment.

2. Put the eggs and sugar in a medium bowl and beat using an electric whisk until well combined and pale. Add the yogurt, oil and vanilla extract and whisk, then fold in the flour, cinnamon and rosemary.

3. Pour the mixture into the prepared tin and spread evenly. Lay the apple slices on top, arranging them in an overlapping circle around the top of the cake until the top is covered.

4. Bake for 30–35 minutes or until risen and it feels spongy and firm and the sides are coming away from tin.

5. Leave the cake to cool in its tin for 5 minutes. Remove from the tin and put on a wire rack to cool. Once the cake has cooled, gently heat the apricot jam then pass it through a sieve to remove lumps. Brush it over the top of the cake.

ORANGE RING CAKE WITH A PISTACHIO NUT GLAZE

Ciambella all'arancia con pistacchi

SERVES 10

80ml full-fat milk
1 vanilla pod
200g salted butter
 (room temperature),
 plus extra for greasing
200g granulated sugar
4 medium eggs
300g self-raising flour
200g cornflour
2 level teaspoons
 baking powder
Pinch of salt
Zest of 1 orange

For the glaze
50g shelled pistachio
 nuts, chopped
100g caster sugar
Juice of 1 orange

The ciambella – a cake in the shape of a ring – originated in the north-eastern region of Emilia-Romagna and is closely related to the *Bundkuchen* (bundt cake) of Austria and Germany. There is no single recipe for this cake and here I decided to use the classic combination of citrus and pistachio. I have also tried this recipe with fresh lemons and it works well too.

1. Preheat the oven to 180°C/gas mark 4. Grease a savarin cake ring tin, 24cm diameter.

2. Pour the milk into a small saucepan. Split the vanilla pod, scrape the seeds into the milk and drop in the pod. Heat over a low heat until warm, stirring. Remove from the heat, leave to infuse for 5 minutes then remove the vanilla pod from the milk.

3. Put the butter, sugar, eggs, flour, cornflour, baking powder, salt and orange zest in a medium bowl and beat using an electric hand whisk until light and fluffy. Stir the milk (with the vanilla seeds) into the flour mixture to combine.

4. Spoon the mixture into the prepared tin and spread it out evenly. Bake for 35–40 minutes or until well risen and the top springs back when lightly pressed.

5. Stand the tin on a cooling rack and leave the cake to cool. Run a knife around the cake and turn it out onto a serving plate.

6. To make the glaze, sieve the pistachios to remove the dusty skins. Put the pistachios, sugar and orange juice in a small pan and heat over a low heat until the sugar dissolves. Gently place the nuts evenly on the cake and carefully spoon over the glaze.

Torta di pere alla Toscana

SERVES 10

Butter (room
  temperature) for
  greasing
280g plain flour
½ teaspoon ground
  cinnamon
¼ teaspoon salt
½ teaspoon baking
  powder
1¼ teaspoons
  bicarbonate of soda
120ml olive oil
190g caster sugar
1 teaspoon vanilla
  extract
2 medium eggs
4 pears, peeled, cored
  and cut into
  1cm cubes
80g raisins
Zest of 1 unwaxed
  lemon
50g pine nuts
2 medium egg whites
Icing sugar for dusting

Pears have been cultivated in Italy for thousands of years, particularly in Tuscany and Umbria. Most varieties in the north ripen in autumn or winter, while those in central Italy tend to ripen earlier – in midsummer. Pears are often used in desserts in Italy, for example stewed with wine or baked in a cake as here. Rocha or Comice pears are perfect for this recipe as they are sweet and juicy and will hold their shape when cooked.

1. Preheat the oven to 180°C/gas mark 4. Grease a traybake tin, measuring 20 x 28cm, and line with baking parchment.

2. Put the flour, cinnamon, salt, baking powder and bicarbonate of soda in a medium bowl. Set aside.

3. Pour the oil into a large bowl, add the sugar and vanilla extract and whisk using an electric hand whisk. Gradually add the eggs, whisking continually until smooth. Fold in the flour mixture using a wooden spoon, then the pears, raisins, lemon zest and pine nuts.

4. In a separate bowl, whisk the egg whites using a balloon whisk or an electric hand whisk on full speed until they form stiff peaks. Fold the egg whites gently into the mixture in 2 batches using a metal spoon, being careful not to knock out all the air.

5. Tip the mixture into the prepared tin and spread evenly. Bake for 25–30 minutes or until risen and the sides shrink from the sides of the tin. Dust with icing sugar.

CHESTNUT CAKE WITH CHOCOLATE AND WHIPPED CREAM

Castagnaccio cioccolato e panna montata

SERVES 10

100g salted butter
  (room temperature),
  plus extra for greasing
150g chestnut flour
125g light brown
  muscovado sugar
4 medium eggs
2 level teaspoons
  baking powder
100g dark chocolate
  chips
250ml double or
  whipping cream
1 tablespoon icing
  sugar
Dark chocolate drops
  to decorate
Cocoa powder to
  decorate

Originally from Tuscany, chestnut cake was once considered a poor man's dessert. It was usually made in late autumn and early winter – once the chestnut crop had been harvested and turned into flour – and was made from local, seasonal and often foraged ingredients. Here I've given the cake a huge overhaul into the 21st century and devised a simple recipe that oozes with dark chocolate. The chestnut flour imparts a lovely earthy flavour.

1. Preheat the oven to 160°C/gas mark 3. Grease a deep, loose-bottomed round cake tin, 20cm diameter, and line with baking parchment.

2. Sift the chestnut flour into a medium bowl. (Don't skip this step as the flour can contain gritty bits.) Add the sugar, butter, eggs and baking powder and whisk using an electric hand whisk for about 2 minutes or until smooth. Fold in the chocolate chips.

3. Spoon the mixture into the prepared tin and spread evenly. Bake for 35 minutes or until risen and the sides shrink from the sides of the tin. Remove from the oven and leave the cake to cool in its tin.

4. Just before serving put the cream in a bowl and whip using a balloon whisk or an electric hand whisk on low speed until it forms soft peaks. Fold in the icing sugar. Cut the cake into slices and place a spoonful of whipped cream on each slice. Scatter over chocolate drops and sprinkle over cocoa powder.

A NOTE FROM THE AUTHOR

Making a successful programme is all about team work – and making a great programme is all about working with a great team. I guess you can probably tell that I think *Gino's Italian Escape: Hidden Italy* is a great programme! I'm a very lucky guy to have been able to travel around my beautiful homeland and show you some of its wonderful hidden treasures, but I couldn't have done it without the fantastic hard work, long hours and amazing skills of this bunch of lunatics ... sorry, professionals!

From left to right: Francesco Molteni (runner), Katy Ross (home economist), Laura D'Alberto (production coordinator), Abbi-Rose Crook (hair and make-up artist), Alison Ercolani (fixer), Gino, Justin Frahm (director of photography), Naveed Chowdhary-Flatt (series producer & director), Kurt Howard (sound recordist), Paola Desiderio (assistant producer), Melissa White (assistant photographer), Hal Shinnie (photographer).